Teaching Basic Skills to Students with Learning Difficulties

Jeanne Sutcliffe

ALBSU
Registered Charity No. 1003969

The Basic
Skills Unit

NIACE

THE NATIONAL ORGANISATION
FOR ADULT LEARNING

Acknowledgements

I would like to thank all of the staff and people with learning difficulties who shared their work and ideas with me. I would also like to thank Jim Pateman (ALBSU), Alan Tuckett (NIACE), Anne Agius (NIACE) and Ken Simons (Norah Fry Research Centre) for their support and encouragement.

© The Adult Literacy and Basic Skills Unit
7th Floor, Commonwealth House, 1-19 New Oxford Street, London WC1A 1NU.

Published March 1994

ISBN 1 85990 000 3

Design: Studio 21

24.10.94

Contents

Chapter 1
Preparing to start   7

Chapter 2
Planning learning programmes with students   23

Chapter 3
Selecting learning materials   43

Chapter 4
Learning in action   54

Chapter 5
Getting started – ideas for communication, literacy and numeracy   63

Chapter 6
Developing themes and projects   99

Chapter 7
Evaluation, accreditation and progression   113

Appendix   124

Preface

Who is this book for?

This book is aimed particularly at people new to teaching basic skills to adults with learning difficulties in a variety of settings:

- Part time tutors, volunteers and full time staff teaching in colleges, adult education centres and training schemes.

- Staff and volunteers working in Social Services, Health Authority, private or voluntary services such as:
  - Day centres and services
  - Hostels and group homes
  - Employment schemes.

The book may also be of interest to parents, relatives and carers of adults with learning difficulties.

The book is designed to support people working towards ALBSU Standards for Basic Skills Teachers (1992, ALBSU).

Note to readers

Readers of this book are likely to come from different backgrounds. It may be that you are already a basic skills tutor or volunteer and that you are going to start working with adults with learning difficulties for the first time. On the other hand, perhaps you regularly work or spend time with adults with learning difficulties but are new to teaching basic skills. Some of you will be new both to working with adults with learning difficulties, and to teaching basic skills. This book is designed to address the needs of all three groups of people and recognises that each may have different perspectives and experiences to build on.

CHAPTER 1

Preparing to start

Introduction

> *"I've been learning to read for fourteen years. I'm getting bored with it now!"*

It is often assumed that adults with learning difficulties must learn to read and write in order to be more independent. There is frequently pressure from parents, relatives and staff who firmly believe it to be in an individual's best interests. Sometimes adults with learning difficulties internalise this belief, and say that literacy and numeracy are what they most want to learn. However, when presented with a full range of learning experiences, most adults with learning difficulties will choose widely – from yoga to bricklaying.

Literacy and numeracy are not appropriate options for all adults with learning difficulties.

Clive enjoys woodwork and family life. He is married with a young child. His wife wanted him to learn to read. His social worker thought it would be important for him to learn to read. His parents thought it would be a very good idea. Clive has now had two abortive attempts at learning to read over the years with 1:1 tuition from experienced tutors. Both attempts failed miserably because Clive himself was not at all motivated to learn to read. As he said, "I'd rather be doing my woodwork."

Unless people are motivated to learn to read, there is little point in trying to teach them – whatever other people say.

Getting by without literacy and numeracy

Many adults with learning difficulties get by perfectly well without literacy and numeracy, and have developed strategies to cope accordingly. James, who lives independently, says:

> *"My social worker or my neighbours help me with reading any letters I get."*

Sarah travels independently by bus to her self advocacy group and to her part-time job. The fact that she cannot read the timetable is not a barrier:

> *"I just ask people what the time is and when the next bus is coming."*

Graham draws pictures to take shopping instead of a written list. Rather than assuming that all adults with learning difficulties automatically need literacy and numeracy skills to be developed, we should be asking critically: does this person really want to develop literacy and numeracy skills? If so, for what particular purpose?

Learning or "Containment" – a dumping ground?

Literacy and numeracy classes have in some areas become a dumping ground, where people with learning difficulties can end up for years on end without making any progress. In some cases, a casual approach to planning and participation causes chaos. A co-ordinator writes:

> *"We are continually aware of examples which bear little resemblance to planned and structured programmes of learning but look much more like 'containment activity'. In some instances three people are expected; it occasionally appears that any three will do."*

Of course there are examples of good practice too, but in a sense this book has been inspired by some of the grey areas in basic skills work with adults with learning difficulties. As one co-ordinator said: "Our tutors think that if you're nice to the students, and they enjoy themselves, that's enough. We think that's about caring, not learning."

People with learning difficulties – who are we talking about?

Adults with learning difficulties have in the past been described as being "slow learners" or having "mental handicaps". The use of the term "learning difficulties" in this book follows its usage in legislation such as the Further & Higher Education Act (1992), and also respects the preferences of many adults with learning difficulties themselves, as recent research shows (Simons, 1993). People may have moderate, severe or profound and complex learning difficulties. However, labels or IQ scores do not tell us anything about a person's strengths or interests. We can only establish those by getting to know an individual.

Getting to know someone with learning difficulties

It can be daunting to consider teaching adults with learning difficulties if you have not met anyone with learning difficulties before. One volunteer describes her anxiety on first meeting her student:

> *"I'm ashamed to admit it now, but I was scared stiff! Peter was huge – over 6 feet tall – and bearded. There we were in a multi-storey car park on our own. I was petrified he might attack me! Now I've got to know him, I realise he's very gentle."*

Myths and prejudices are rife, and there is still confusion between mental illness and learning difficulties. People sometimes mistakenly fear that adults with learning difficulties will be violent.

If you are new to working with adults with learning difficulties, you may want to do some background reading. "Know Me As I Am" is an anthology of writing, poetry and art by individuals with learning difficulties, which offers insights into their lives, experiences and perspectives.

You may want to spend time getting to know someone with learning difficulties as an individual. Some people have:

- offered time to a citizen advocacy scheme. Citizen advocates are paired with adults with learning difficulties one to one and help to represent their partner's interest, as well as offering friendship and support.

- supported an adult with learning difficulties to join an ordinary adult education class, for example yoga or computing. Shared interests are a good way of getting to know each other.

Avoiding the "zoo" syndrome

Visits to huge day centres for adults with learning difficulties or to large-scale social clubs (such as Gateway clubs) are not a good way to get to know adults with learning difficulties. Seeing people with learning difficulties en masse in big groups in segregated settings for a fleeting visit is a bit like going to the zoo. Getting to know a person or a group on equal terms over a period of time is a much better idea.

What can we expect?

Adults with learning difficulties are likely to have gaps in their knowledge (like all of us!) and to learn more slowly than other people. The main challenge for tutors is that people with learning difficulties often have trouble in generalising their learning. For example, a student may recognise the number 47 on a flashcard in the classroom, but may have difficulty recognizing it in another context, such as in a different colour or type face on the front of a bus. This factor makes it essential to continually relate learning to real life situations. Adults with learning difficulties frequently have problems in learning spontaneously, which means that tutors need to plan their teaching in a systematic and structured way. In addition, some adults with learning difficulties may have one or more of the following:

- an additional physical disability. Some adults with learning difficulties have limited physical mobility, and some use wheelchairs

- a sensory impairment affecting eyesight, hearing or sometimes both. These may not have been recognised. For example, it may be many years since the students have had their eyes tested; all too often the problems people experience are automatically attributed to their learning difficulty

- speech or communication difficulties.

Additional disabilities or difficulties such as these are bound to affect teaching and learning strategies (see Chapter 4.) A very small proportion of adults with learning difficulties are described as having "challenging" behaviour which poses a threat to themselves or to others. For example, one group regularly receives basic skills tuition on the secure ward of the long stay hospital where they are resident. The tutors who work with these students are highly experienced and have chosen to work in a secure setting.

Self advocacy and "People First" groups
It is important to remember that adults with learning difficulties are above all people first.

Self advocacy is a process whereby adults with learning difficulties speak up and work for change, both individually and collectively. There are a growing number of self advocacy groups and courses for adults with learning difficulties.

The self advocacy movement has clearly demonstrated that many adults with learning difficulties are able to or can learn to speak up and make choices and decisions. Some people have progressed to influence policy and to speak at and run conferences. A number of independent groups called "People First" exist, while other self advocacy groups and courses operate in many areas (see the resources list at the end of this chapter for relevant reading and addresses.)

Adult and continuing education has played an important role in the development of self advocacy. A number of People First groups have their origins in basic skills groups.

Tutors can help by providing opportunities for students to talk about their lives, taking people seriously, and valuing what they say. Helping people change things for the better may sometimes be an important part of a basic skills course. For example, one group living in a hostel revealed how unhappy they were with the behaviour of some staff. The group looked at how the local authority complaints procedure worked and together wrote a letter of complaint. The complaint was duly investigated and some of the staff were suspended.

Discussion and communication skills slots as part of basic skills can help adults with learning difficulties to practice speaking up, while choice and decision making should be an inbuilt part of the curriculum.

An ordinary life

"An ordinary life" is something most of us take for granted. For adults with learning difficulties, their disability may have resulted in:

- separate, "special" schooling, away from their local neighbourhood

- placement at a day centre, where groups of adults with learning difficulties are sometimes effectively segregated from the rest of society

- placement in a long stay hospital. With the move to care in the community, it is now accepted that adults with learning difficulties have the right to live in ordinary housing. However, in March 1992, in England alone there were still 19,600 adults with learning difficulties in long stay hospitals, awaiting the chance to move into the community (Collins, 1993).

Being treated as an adult

Being treated as an adult and having the chance to participate in learning activities can confer a sense of value and self esteem.

Staff at one day centre knew when Simon was starting at college. He appeared at the centre wearing a suit and carrying a brief case . . .

An adult approach is of paramount importance. Respect for people's adult status, rights and dignity should be reflected in the way we talk to and work with adults with learning difficulties.

11

Positive and adult relationships can be encouraged by:

- really listening and valuing what students have to say or communicate

- ensuring that you are using adult materials, or late teenage where appropriate

- working with students to plan learning programmes as equal partners rather than dictating what they should be learning. This process usually involves negotiation between the tutor and the student. Tutors need to listen carefully to what students want as individuals, but to recognise that the inevitable pressures of time, resources, student numbers or sheer practical arrangements may mean that a negotiated compromise is reached.

It is not acceptable to treat people as children or to use pre-school or primary school materials such as cardboard clocks, plastic money or coloured bricks (see Chapter 3 for details of adult materials).

"Not in front of the students"

Talking to others about students with learning difficulties in their presence is not acceptable, unless you are saying positive things and involving the students in the discussion. It may be stating the obvious, but it does need saying. Some adults with learning difficulties have low self esteem and poor self image, which will only be reinforced if negative comments are overheard. The following unfortunate comments have all been made in front of students:

> *"Gavin doesn't give much, does he?"* (Tutor)

> *"I've been specially trained to work with people who are mental, dear."*
> (Volunteer tutor)

> *"Sunita can't sew at all. She can't do anything right. She'll never learn."* (Parent).

The cycle of low expectations and negative labels and images is reinforced by comments like these which are heard and absorbed by the individuals concerned.

Integration versus segregation: the big debate

Should adults with learning difficulties study basic skills in special groups set up for them, or should they join groups and learn alongside adults without disabilities? This is a difficult question, and something of a hot potato.

In terms of equal opportunities, of course adults with learning difficulties should have access to mainstream provision. However, there are a number of difficulties which relate particularly to basic skills provision (for a discussion of integration in other contexts see the NIACE publication "Integration for Adults with Learning Difficulties"):

- If more than one or two adults with learning difficulties join an established basic skills group, the load may be too much for the tutor. He or she will already be working out individual programmes, and to cope with more than one or two particularly slow learners is hard.

- Adults who do not have learning difficulties, but who do have problems with literacy and numeracy are likely to have low confidence and self esteem. To be in a group with several people who obviously have severe learning difficulties can make people feel uncomfortable to the point of thinking: "They must think I have severe learning difficulties too."

This book cannot set out any clear answers, because local situations vary so much. However, some advice can be gleaned from visits and observation:

- Consideration should be given to the optimum number of adults with learning difficulties to be integrated into any one basic skills class. Students should have additional support within the class if necessary.

- Segregated or "closed" groups should ideally meet in a community setting where there are opportunities to meet other learners. There should be the chance to move on from that provision (See chapter 7).

- Integration is a two way process. In some cases, adults from basic skills groups have elected to join groups for adults with learning difficulties because they preferred the slower pace.

Basic skills in action for adults with learning difficulties

These brief snapshots of students learning illustrate the range and diversity of basic skills provision for adults with learning difficulties:

A college part time course

Caroline has Down's syndrome and is on a course where she attends college for 21 hours a week. For part of this time, she works towards individual goals which she has set herself, such as writing her name and address. Negotiating her own programme with the tutor has been an important part of the course.

A drop in open learning centre

Neil has learnt the bus route to a city open learning centre. He works in a small group of between 4 and 6 students. He is on a fixed term course and is taking the "Wordpower" Certificate in Communication Skills at Foundation Level.

Health funded transport training

Sunita is learning to use the bus – to tell which number bus to catch, to pay the fare and when/where to get on and off. A nursing assistant is teaching her.

A voluntary organisation

A community centre hosts a course for adults with learning difficulties run by a small voluntary organisation. Raymond is helping in the centre cafe to improve his numeracy and social skills.

A self advocacy course

Bethan goes to a "speaking for yourself" course at her local community education centre. Developing confidence in communicating is an important part of what she is learning.

A day centre group

Sarah is part of a social services day centre group which meets regularly for creative writing, lead by the centre staff. The group have produced booklets of poetry.

A hospital

Peter studies at a hospital adult education centre which offers a range of basic skills courses to residents – from language development and self advocacy to the Open University "Working Together" course (P555M). Peter is learning to express choices about his life by using photographs as an aid to communication.

A horticultural unit

Raj is a student at a horticultural unit which offers a vocational qualification for adults with learning difficulties. Although much of the course relates to horticulture, some of the content relates particularly to basic skills. Raj has been potting up plants and learning to use a kettle.

A private home

Rachel lives in a private home, where staff have taken the ALBSU Initial Certificate in Teaching Basic Skills (9282). They teach the one or two residents who want to improve their writing and reading, including Rachel.

A training cafe

Michael works at a cafe which offers adults with learning difficulties the chance to do employment training. Weighing ingredients, making and pricing food, taking orders and working out bills are just some of the basic skills they learn "on the job".

An English for Speakers of Other Languages (ESOL) group

Vimal went to school in India and came to England as a teenager. She attends a community based English for Speakers of Other Languages (ESOL) group with her mother.

Basic skills across the curriculum

It is important to recognise that basic skills provide the foundation for a wide range of learning opportunities. Consider some of the basic skills required in a couple of subjects:

Woodwork

- Measuring wood
- Reading or following instructions
- Counting screws or nails
- Recognising tools
- Health and safety awareness.

Cookery

- Weighing or measuring ingredients
- Reading a recipe or following oral or taped instructions
- Sequencing of instructions
- Setting an oven at the right temperature.

Communication, literacy and numeracy are all a part of most subjects. The basic skills tutor needs to provide tuition which links coherently with other learning which the student is undertaking. In some cases, linked skills classes are offered, where by literacy, numeracy and oral communication skills are taught in relation to a particular practical subject. In other cases, the tutor will need to do some background homework to find out what basic skills tuition would most appropriately support other skills being learnt by the student with learning difficulties. Sometimes the best route will be to liase with the tutors of other courses, with the consent of the student. We have to recognise that some basic skills tuition is best done as a part of other education and training, rather than being offered separately. For example, for students who are learning for work, basic skills tasks relevant to their activities (whether counting photocopies or putting the right stamps on envelopes) will be more effectively learnt in the context of their jobs or employment experience than in a separate class.

A word to basic skills tutors

For people who have taught basic skills for a while, but who are new to working with adults with learning difficulties, here is some advice offered by co-ordinating tutors:

"It's just the same as teaching adult basic education. You just have to break the tasks down more and make the steps smaller. There's no mystique."

"Most adult basic education materials can be adapted for students who have learning difficulties. Indeed, tutors would need to adapt most materials according to the experience and needs of any group of students."

"Basic skills tutors . . . should consider how to enable students who have learning difficulties to plan, draft and edit their writing, how to enable them to select relevant texts and read with understanding and how to enable them to communicate more effectively and to deal with the numeracy demands of their lives. We have found that on their own, separate severe learning difficulties (tutor) training courses can reinforce prejudices such as "But my students are different", "Spelling is not relevant to severe learning difficulties students", etc."

16

Working across agencies

It is vital that various agencies collaborate to develop basic skills for adults with learning difficulties. Otherwise, the progress made can be minimal:

> Alex has been doing a literacy class at her day centre and a literacy class at college. The two classes are run separately, and the tutors (one from the college and one from social services) don't have the time or the occasion to liaise. They have never met.
>
> Alex's folder is crammed full of repeated worksheets. For five years she has been doing the same worksheets at the centre . . . and again at the college. She is now understandably fed up with the repetition, and is feeling bad that she has not made any real progress: "I can't seem to get on with this!"

Involving other professionals

Many adults with learning difficulties have numerous professionals involved with them in different capacities. It may be useful to liaise with key personnel to effectively co-ordinate learning programmes.

However, it is important to respect the student's wishes on this matter. Confidentiality and privacy are vital.

As one student said after visiting the careers office: "How did they know about my epilepsy? I didn't tell them. Bloody cheek!" However, if students wish other professionals to be involved, you may find yourself working alongside one or more of the following:

- Social workers from day centres and services, homes and hostels or field social work teams
- Occupational therapists
- Nurses from community teams or long stay hospitals
- Physiotherapists
- Speech therapists
- Group home staff

- Adult and further education staff
- Employment schemes
- Psychiatrists
- Psychologists
- Dieticians.

For example, when Freda and Alec got married, they needed to learn to cook. A community nurse and an adult education tutor jointly worked out a programme combining literacy and cookery, backed up by a dietician. The couple were taught intensively in their home, and also attended evening classes.

Graham is going to an integrated Indian cookery evening class. His literacy tutor works with him on recipes that he is using. This enables Graham to practise reading and sequencing skills; reinforces what he has learnt, and also prepares him for the coming week's cookery class.

Involving parents, relatives and carers

Not all of us want our families closely involved in our learning. I for one used to cry when my older sister tried to teach me maths!

However, it is important to bear in mind that some adults with learning difficulties may want to involve someone at home to back up their learning. Where the person selected (by the adult with learning difficulties) is willing, this can provide a use ful way of reinforcing and consolidating learning.

Involving peers

Sometimes friends may gladly take on a support role:

> Carol attends a day centre. She is reasonably competent at reading and writing. She is glad to be able to help those people less skilled than her to develop their literacy skills.

> Douglas lives in a long stay hospital. One of his friends in the adult education class taught him how to use a tape recorder. His friend has no speech, but demonstrated how to do it.

Getting ready to start

When you are getting ready to teach basic skills to adults with learning difficulties, there are a number of questions and issues to address beforehand:

Where will your support and training come from?

Ask if there is a suitable training course in your area. In some places, the ALBSU Certificate in Teaching Basic Skills is offered to staff from different agencies.

You will certainly want a key person to support your work, especially at the beginning, but also on an ongoing basis. In one area, people learn to teach basic skills to adults with learning difficulties alongside more experienced tutors, on a sort of apprenticeship model.

Where will your resources come from?

You will need access to basic materials. Chapter 3 deals in detail with the sorts of resources you may went to use. It is important to establish early on:

- What resources are available?
- Where are they kept?
- How can you access them?
- Who will supply basic stationery, such as paper, folders, pens and pencils?
- Is there a safe place where you can keep materials in between sessions?

These questions are important for all basic skills tutors, but are especially pertinent for tutors working in different settings with adults with learning difficulties. You may, for example, find yourself working in the space of one week in a Further Education college, a Social Services day centre and a Health Authority hospital. All three establishments may have different ideas about who should pay for basic equipment and resources. To resolve these questions in advance will save frustrations such as:

- a day centre classroom having a well stocked resources cupboard which always seems to be locked when you are there

- a hospital where to do a quick photocopy just before a class involves a trek to the other side of the site and filling out a form in triplicate.

You may find that you have no option but to carry resources and materials around with you, especially if you work on several sites.

Who will your students be?

All students need an individual interview to determine what they want to learn. This is an ALBSU Quality Mark standard. It is up to you as a tutor to make sure that this has happened. This will ideally mean arranging to meet with individuals before tuition begins. As described in the opening section, adults with learning difficulties are often pressurised into basic skills classes. Talking informally with students once they have relaxed with you is one way to explore their motivation, and to check that they have not been pressured into attending by other people such as staff or relatives.

Where will you work?

Whether you are going into a day centre, college or hospital as a tutor, you will want to negotiate a good place to work in if you can. This means looking for a room that is:

- quiet and well lit
- wheelchair accessible if necessary
- preferably stocked with basic skills resources, or which at least has space for storing materials.

In the interests of giving adults with learning difficulties the chance to mix with other learners, it is preferable to site classes in adult education centres and colleges rather than in segregated day centres, hostels and hospitals. However, it is not always possible to do this for practical reasons such as transport. One group from a day centre meets in a library within walking distance, which provides a convenient base, sited in an ordinary community setting and with plenty of materials to hand.

Difficulties with a place to work can cause frustrations. Experiences such as those described below reveal that adults with learning difficulties are still often marginalised and excluded by negative attitudes. What strategies could you use to deal with these two situations?

One group from a day centre regularly arrived at college to find their wheelchair accessible base room had been occupied by another class. Their weekly use of the room was not viewed as a priority by the college timetablers.

The tutor of one basic skills group meeting in a day centre staff room (the only available space) was asked not to use the table. The deputy manager explained "We have to eat our lunch off that table, you see!" In fact, the group used to wipe up tea, coffee and biscuit crumbs left by the staff before they could start work.

Getting ready to start: a checklist

▶ Have you identified relevant training courses in your area? ☐

▶ Have you identified a key person to support your work? ☐

▶ Have you found a good source of resources? ☐

▶ Have you established who will provide basic stationery? ☐

▶ Have you found a good room to work in – and booked it? ☐

▶ Have you negotiated a safe place to store materials and folders in between sessions? ☐

▶ Have you had an initial interview with individual students to find out what they want to learn and to make sure that they really want to learn basic skills? ☐

Resources
General
Adults with learning difficulties: Education for choice and empowerment, Jeannie Sutcliffe, (1990, Open University Press/NIACE).

Self advocacy
Self Advocacy and Adults with Learning Difficulties – Contexts and Debates, Jeannie Sutcliffe & Ken Simons (1993, NIACE).

"Sticking up for yourself" Self advocacy and people with learning difficulties, Ken Simons (1993, Joseph Rowntree Foundation/Community Care).

A full resource listing about self advocacy is available from: Andrea Whittaker, King's Fund Centre 126 Albert Street LONDON NW1 7NF Tel: 071-267 6111.

Citizen advocacy
Citizen Advocacy: The Inside View, Ken Simons (1993, Norah Fry Research Centre).

Details of local schemes can be obtained from: National Citizen Advocacy Resource & Advisory Centre, Unit 2K, Leroy House, 436 Essex Road, LONDON N1 3QP. Tel: 071-359 8289.

References
Know Me As I Am – An anthology of prose, poetry and art by people with learning difficulties, (1990, Hodder and Stoughton).

The Resettlement Game – Policy and Procrastination in the Closure of Mental Handicap Hospitals, Jean Collins, (1993, Values Into Action).

Integration for Adults with Learning Difficulties, Jeannie Sutcliffe (1992, NIACE).

CHAPTER 2

Planning learning programmes with students

This chapter offers a summary and overview of how to plan learning programmes with students who have learning difficulties. For an in depth analysis of the skills required, you may wish to consult the ALBSU Standards for Basic Skills Teachers. This document offers a structured framework for assessing and developing the competences needed by tutors. It has core sections on identifying learning needs, designing learning programmes, providing learning opportunities and evaluating learning. It provides the basis for the joint ALBSU/City and Guilds Certificate in Teaching Basic Skills (9285). This is the current qualification for tutors working with basic skills students. Some readers may already have this certificate, while others may be interested to find out more about it.

Assessment

In the past, assessment has tended to be a process done to rather than with adults with learning difficulties. Detailed, quasi-scientific checklists and diagrams have been used to objectively assess people. The problem with this approach is that:

- it distances adults with learning difficulties from the process

- it tends to highlight deficits – what people *can't* do

- the items on checklists may be of little relevance to people's real lives and situations.

A profile building on strengths and interests: I can and I want to

A better approach builds on the strengths and interests of students:

- Talk with people about what they can do

- Ask students to think about what they want to do

- Record the information together. Use pictures or photos or a tape recorder if it helps

- Students should keep copies of their strengths and interests profiles. An example of one is given on page 24.

I CAN AND I WANT TO

I CAN

Tell the time

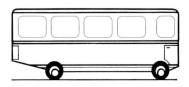

Catch a bus

Write my name
and address

I WANT TO

Give the right money
in the coffee bar

Tell what's on my
tapes and records

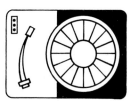

Write to my brother
in Australia

Why Assess?

Assessment gives a starting point from which to plan learning programmes. It is vital to use the material and information from assessments to inform planning. Too often tutors spend so long assessing adults with learning difficulties that they never get to teach anything! Sometimes the information is stored in filing cabinets and never touched. A system which enables the students with learning difficulties to keep control of their records is much better. Naturally, the tutor will want to keep records too – or else a shared system can be developed.

Assessment can be used for three purposes:

- to give an early picture of strengths, needs and interests, and to identify priorities for learning
- to periodically assess progress during the course of a period of learning.
- to establish progress at the end of a course.

You will almost certainly find that you are surprised by some of the developing pictures of students' strengths and needs. Development in the areas of literacy, numeracy and communication can be patchy and uneven, as the following examples show:

> Wendy can barely write her name, and cannot read letters or words. However, she enjoys maths and can easily add and subtract to 20 with a number line (which has the numbers 1 to 20 written out in sequence).

> Stephen is very articulate and lives independently. He is unable to read and write. He uses pictures which he draws to remind him what he needs when he goes shopping.

> Sarah is quiet and shy, and does not say much. Her poor communication skills led her tutor to suspect initially that her literacy skills would also be limited. In fact, Sarah can read and write well and has written her life story.

Practical hints – assessment and planning learning programmes

- Keep it simple
- Involve the students

- Make sure the students have copies of assessments/learning plans in a format accessible to them

- This may mean using photos, pictures or a tape; or the students dictating their thoughts to you.

Remember that students may well have limited concentration spans. Several short learning sessions are likely to be more effective than one prolonged one.

Linking in with other assessments

It is likely that the adults with learning difficulties you are working with will have already been assessed and be working towards goals which have been set as part of individual planning processes in Health, Social Services or independent sector organisations. In different areas, these are sometimes call individual programme plans (IPPs) or life plans. A few areas use a process called Shared Action Planning, developed by Brechin & Swain.

It may be that, with your student's permission and co-operation, you will want to link your learning programmes to co-ordinate with goals that have already been set. Basic skills tutors are sometimes asked to contribute reports or to attend multi-disciplinary IPP or review meetings.

Your students may also be coming for basic skills support as part of a college course, for example in catering. In this case it would be important that the areas you identify to work on include the basic skills required for the particular course.

A word of warning

While it can be very positive to work alongside other professionals and with students with learning difficulties towards set goals, there can be pitfalls to look out for:

- Large groups of professionals at IPP meetings can often silence and disempower adults with learning difficulties

- Other people working with adults with learning difficulties may have different ideas about priorities and approaches

- The student with learning difficulties may want information about their abilities and progress to be kept confidential

- Sometimes people with learning difficulties are routinely referred for literacy tuition "because they can't read" or "because it's on their IPP". This does not guarantee that the student (or potential student) is willing or motivated.

Self assessment

Asking students to assess themselves and to keep records of their own learning enables them to be fully involved, and to have ownership of their learning.

- It can take time for some adults with learning difficulties to get used to the idea of expressing their learning needs. Time for negotiation and thinking things through will be essential.

- Offering open choices may be too overwhelming at first for those students who have had little experience of making decisions. You will find that you can create situations in which students can gradually develop the skills to direct their own learning. It is a process with small steps, that can be difficult at times. You may find the following strategies helpful:

  - initially offering guided choices, where you make suggestions and the student chooses between one or two options

  - then offering a wider choice of activities and materials with the student making more of the decisions

  - finally encouraging the student to take responsibility for their own learning choices.

In this way, there can be shift of balance over time, with the tutor input gradually decreasing.

- Putting a wide range of learning materials out and letting students choose will give an indication of interests and levels, without putting pressure on them.

Setting aims and objectives

An **aim** is a general statement of intent, for example:

"I want to do more for myself – be independent."

"I want to learn about money."

"I want to go to the cinema."

27

An **objective** is a specific goal which is narrowed down, from the broad aim:

> *"I want to catch the number 47 bus."*

> *"I want to tell the difference between £10 and £20 notes."*

> *"I want to know what money to give for a cinema ticket."*

Objectives should be targets which are tangible, specific and which can be observed.

Objectives can be further broken down into small steps, as in the catching the bus example:

I want to:

- find the right bus stop
- recognise which bus to get on
- pay for my ticket
- get off at the right place.

Breaking down learning into small steps is a useful way of analysing the component skills of a task. This is called task analysis. Task analysis breaks tasks down into observable competencies (or "can do" statements). This approach relates well to the emerging role of competence based qualifications. For example, basic skills achievements can be demonstrated by pieces of work which can be used to build up credits for accreditation schemes such as Wordpower or Numberpower (see also Chapter 7). The bus journey example of task analysis is further broken down on page 29, with points for reflection added by the tutor. In this particular instance, it would be necessary to think through:

Risk taking

- Is the student allowed to go out independently?
- Does advice, or permission need to be sought from family or staff?
- Will the student need shadowing until he/she has learnt the journey? Who can do this?
- If you are restricted to classroom work, is there a volunteer/relative/another staff member who could do the actual travel training, leaving you to concentrate on the back up work?

Preparation and follow up activities

This could include taking photos of the route and landmarks for practice and sequencing of the journey.

Relevance to student's life

Is this bus journey one which the student will really make use of in his/her everyday life?

Catching the number 47 bus	
Steps involved	*Tutor's points for follow up and discussion with student*
1. Walk to bus stop	<ul><li>Check route.</li><li>Check road safety awareness of student.</li><li>Follow up if needed.</li><li>Check for landmarks/social signs on the way.</li><li>Look at timetables.</li></ul>
2. Wait for the 47 bus	<ul><li>Check recognition of colour and type of bus – minibus? single decker? double decker?</li><li>Check recognition of the number 47 (& route destination if student can read).</li></ul>
3. Get on bus	<ul><li>Check physical mobility of student.</li><li>Talk through scenario – what to do if the bus does not come.</li></ul>
4. Ask for fare and/or destination	<ul><li>How much is the fare?</li><li>Is it a "correct fare" only service?</li><li>What coins/notes should the student offer?</li></ul>
5. Sit down and travel to chosen destination	<ul><li>How can you tell when you have arrived?</li><li>What landmarks are there?</li></ul>
6. Get off bus	<ul><li>What do you do if you miss your stop?</li></ul>
7. Continue journey by foot to final destination	<ul><li>Are directions needed?</li><li>How many roads need to be crossed and where are the safest crossing points?</li></ul>

Learning to catch the 47 bus without a clear purpose in mind is meaningless. Can the skills be generalised to other routes and destinations?

Why record learning?

Recording learning is useful because it gives a framework for planning sessions and reviewing progress. It helps to record:

- what the student wants to learn, and how (see Planning learning: a student record sheet on this page)

- how each session went (see Recording learning: a student record sheet on page 31).

Students unable to write can dictate their views and feelings. Student unable to speak may be able to communicate by sign, symbol or gesture. Simple pictures of happy, unhappy or neutral faces can also help those with limited literacy skills to express how they feel about learning. Where more than one tutor is working with a student, thought needs to be given to the most appropriate way of sharing record keeping.

Planning learning: a student record sheet	
What do you want to learn?	• More about shopping
How are you going to do it?	• Go shopping • Practise shopping words and sums
Who would you like to involve?	• My teacher • My key worker at the centre • My mum
How will you check your learning?	• See if I can go by myself with a list and some money
How long do you want to spend on this?	• Till Christmas
(Tutor adds – one term. Many adults with learning difficulties have difficulty with the concept of time).	

Recording learning: a record sheet

Name: ....

Activity

.... Shopping ....

Things I need to practice

	Date	How I got on
Making lists		
Adding up bills with a calculator		

What I need to do next

....

....

....

....

Basic skills: a checklist for self assessment

Tutors can work through these headings with students to help identify possible areas for learning programmes in basic skills.

Apart from ticking off 'can do' competencies, there is scope to discuss what students would like to do that they cannot do at present; and to enable students to prioritise for themselves. Of course, they may well want to learn or practice specific skills not listed – for example, reading the titles of records or tapes or writing up the minutes of a self advocacy meeting. The checklists should be seen as a starting point for discussion and are not designed to be prescriptive.

About me

My name is .... □

I like .... □

I don't like .... □

My interests and hobbies are .... □

I want to come to classes to .... □

Speaking up

I can

Listen to people talking .... □

Talk to one person .... □

Take turns in a conversation .... □

Say how I feel about things .... □

Speak on the telephone .... □

Speak up in a group .... □

Give a talk to a group .... □

I would also like to speak up .... □

I can write

My name and address .... ☐

Letters of the alphabet .... ☐

Greetings cards and postcards .... ☐

Notes and letters .... ☐

Shopping lists and other lists .... ☐

About my life .... ☐

Poems and stories .... ☐

I can

Fill in forms .... ☐

Write cheques .... ☐

Keep a diary .... ☐

Do the pools .... ☐

Write out menus .... ☐

Other things I would like to write:

....

....

....

I can read

My name and address .... ☐

Words we see around us everyday, such as: WAY IN, PUSH, TOILETS etc. .... ☐

Labels .... ☐

Shopping lists .... ☐

Newspapers .... ☐

Magazines .... ☐

Timetables .... ☐

Recipes .... ☐

Leaflets and brochures .... ☐

Instructions and directions e.g. on a medicine bottle .... ☐

"What's on" – TV, cinema, radio .... ☐

Books .... ☐

Other things I would like to read:

....

....

....

I can use numbers to

Count things .... ☐

Tell the time .... ☐

Recognise coins and notes .... ☐

Go shopping .... ☐

Budget .... ☐

Dial telephone numbers .... ☐

Play games like Bingo .... ☐

Keep a bank or building society account .... ☐

Pay bills .... ☐

Measure things for DIY, cookery or gardening .... ☐

Read timetables .... ☐

Use a calculator .... ☐

Other things I would like to use numbers for:

....

....

....

See Chapter 5 for a more detailed checklist for numeracy. Self assessment checklists can be drawn up with students to suit all kinds of different situations. For example, a self assessment checklist for a student studying basic skills in relation to a work placement serving in a cafe might look like this:

I can:

- Talk to customers .... ☐

- Find out what they want .... ☐

- Take the order, using words or ticking a picture order pad .... ☐

- Add up the bill .... ☐

- Take the money .... ☐

- Work out the change with a calculator .... ☐

- Say good-bye to customers .... ☐

Keeping tabs on learning

You will want to keep your own records for groups of learners.

A possible format for group records is shown on page 40. Often people will be working at different tasks, and you will want to keep track of all the activities and resources needed.

Planning in advance

You will find it useful to make notes and to plan for and with individuals in advance. This gives you and the students an overall plan for several weeks, which is better than lurching from week to week and wondering what you are going to do next! You can still build in flexibility if plans change. Two different plans of work for individuals over five weeks are shown. Repetition and revision are built into both plans to ensure consolidation of learning.

Tutor's notes for an individual plan of work over 5 weeks for Linda H.

Linda has moderate learning difficulties. She has a slight speech impediment and is very shy. Her stated aims are:

▶ to be more confident talking to people

▶ to improve her spelling and letter writing. She wants particularly to write to her family, but also to write letters of application for jobs.

▶ to learn to use the post office.

She is keen to use a computer in her learning.

Apart from the activities outlined below, each week Linda will join in with group work on different topics, and will also do a weekly evaluation in a diary format.

Week 1

● Introduce Linda to rest of group as she is a new student.

● Writing a letter to her aunt.

● Start a personal A-Z spelling dictionary to record new words.

● Ask her to practise at home with look, cover, write, check method *(explained in Chapter 5)*.

● Show Linda how to load software in the computer.

● Computer programme to choose the right spelling to fill the gap.

Week 2

● See if Linda would like to help make the coffee to encourage her to chat informally to other group members.

● Revision of new words from last week.

● Work on addressing envelopes as she is not clear of the lay-out.

● Can she recall how to use the computer? Check.

● See if she would like to use a simple word processing package for her next letter – get Alan (another student) to show her.

Week 3

- Repeat revision of the words Linda is learning to spell.

- Practise a couple of envelopes to see if she's got the hang of it. More work if not.

- Start letter on word processor to her brother in Australia with support from volunteer.

- Log new words arising from letter that she wants to learn to spell.

- Encourage her to practise words at home before next week.

Week 4

- Spelling revision.

- Complete letter to brother on computer with support. How much can she do for herself after last week's session?

- Show Linda how to use the Spellcheck on the computer.

- Write airmail letter for envelope.

- Go to post office and get letter weighed with volunteer, as Linda is unsure of using a post office. Ask them to bring back assorted leaflets.

- Buy stamp and post letter.

Week 5

- Look at leaflets from post office – ask Linda to make a list of things you can get or do at the post office.

- Spelling revision.

- One envelope to address, just to make sure!

- Job application letter on the computer. Talk about different styles for business as opposed to personal letters.

- If Linda feels confident enough, see if she'll talk to individuals in the group and make a list of ideas of where to go to, as people are planning a social evening out.

- Review progress so far with Linda: how does she feel the last 5 weeks have gone? What has she learnt? What does she still need practice at, and what would she like to work on next?

Tutor's notes for an individual plan of work over 5 weeks for Michael

Michael has severe learning difficulties. He attends a day centre and has a work experience placement in a wholefood cafe run by a voluntary agency. He is helping both in the kitchen and in the cafe, which uses a pictorial menu order pad so that reading is not essential for taking orders. Both Michael and his placement supervisor think it would be useful for him to work on kitchen words and safety and basic money skills. Michael's reading is limited to a few words. He can write his name and can copy his address. He can count only to 30.

Week 1

- Assess Michael's money recognition using a selection of real coins and notes. He muddles up 5p and 20p. Find out how/when he uses money and what for: so many students have little or no control over personal money. He regularly buys a cup of coffee and a car magazine from the £5 a week spending money his parents give him.

- Pictorial kitchen safety worksheet: ringing the dangers and talking about them. Find out he's not allowed in the kitchen at home – he can make a cup of tea at the day centre but not at home!

Week 2

- Repeat coin recognition to check findings for consistency. If it's definitely the newer and smaller 5p/20p he confuses, learning activity to sort 5p/20p coins into piles and name them.

- Work on reading specific words found in his workplace kitchen: ON, OFF, DANGER. Use flashcards and social sight photos. Ask supervisor to practise them actually in the kitchen to reinforce.

- Pictorial worksheet on kitchen hygiene: tick or cross which is right or wrong. Includes washing hands, covering cuts etc. Discuss.

Week 3

- Matching 5p and 20p coins to outlines of coins and naming.

- Counting coins: can count in 10s to 30 but unsurprisingly not beyond. Also can't add other coins together. When he's out he always gives a £1 coin or a £5 note and keeps all the change!

- Work on counting beyond 30 to 40 and 50.

- Revision of kitchen words. If learnt, introduce a couple of new ones.

Week 4

- 5p/20p revision

- Counting to 40 or 50 revision. Go beyond if grasped.

- Ask Michael to help sort and count the coffee money to put both coin recognition and counting into a real context.

- Kitchen words revision. As last week – if learning is consolidated, add a couple more words.

- Photos of kitchen objects – knives, cooker, grater, etc. Talk through what could be dangerous about them and what to do if you hurt yourself.

Week 5

- 5p/20p revision – hopefully after this slot he'll just need an occasional reminder.

- Counting revision – aim to get to 100 in the next 5 week teaching slot *if* he's got the hang of it.

- Kitchen words revision. Check progress on reading these in the work place with supervisor. Add new words if appropriate.

- Recap on safety with last week's photos.

- Review progress with Michael. There is a certificate in food hygiene course at the local college with materials for adults with learning difficulties – talk with Michael and his supervisor about this as a possible progression route.

Organising groups

Working with groups in which individuals are pursuing different goals and activities has been compared to plate spinning! The situation can be eased by:

- use of volunteers

- use of co-tutors, possibly from different agencies

- structuring sessions so that more able students can support other learners for part of the time

- setting activities that do not require 1:1 tutor input for all of the time

- group work, whereby the whole group focuses on a particular topic, activity or theme (see also Chapter 6).

Session Plan: Group Record

Name	Individual work before break
Renu	Shopping sums with Miriam
Martin	Working on life story with volunteer
Mary	Writing about her job
Simon	Writing about football
Miriam	Shopping sums with Renu
Ken	Computer work on spelling
Rachel	Computer work on spelling

Group work after break

Discussion and writing about holidays.

All to bring in photos and brochures.

Link in to planning day away at the end of term.

Planning for reinforcement

Revision and reinforcement of learning is essential for consolidation. Planning for practice and repetition should be a part of the learning plan. This means thinking through:

- Is there any homework that the student can do in between sessions?

- Is there someone who can help with this, if need be?

- How can subsequent teaching sessions reinforce the same points without becoming boring – for you or for the student?

Planning for generalisation of skills

Adults with learning difficulties tend not to transfer their learning easily. For example, a photograph of a social sign such as "Way in" may not be related to the actual real life setting in a supermarket.

This makes it important to practise skills in a variety of settings, and to make sure that if practical skills are being worked on – such as using a calculator – the student has access to a similar model outside of the classroom. Better still, he or she could bring one in to use.

Task sheet

▶ Try out task analysis for yourself!

▶ Look at some everyday activities and see how many small steps are involved in:
  – making a cup of tea
  – making a train journey
  – looking up a phone number.

▶ Which components relate directly to basic skills – communication, literacy and numeracy?

▶ Think about the pre-requisite skills that are necessary, before these tasks are tackled. Are there short cuts which can be made, such as ringing to make an enquiry if you can't read? What similar "short cuts" would help your students?

▶ What assessment procedures have you come across for adults with learning difficulties?

▶ What are the pros and cons of the systems you have found? How much do they focus on the needs of each individual student? How much of what you do is dictated by other factors (e.g. pressure on time/lack of resources)?

Checklist

- What do you understand by the term:

  needs? .... ☐

  assessment? .... ☐

  aims? .... ☐

  objectives? .... ☐

  task analysis? .... ☐

  competence? .... ☐

- Have you decided how to assess your students? .... ☐

- Have you devised ways of enabling students to assess their own learning
  needs? .... ☐

- Have you prepared sheets to record learning plans for groups and for
  individuals? .... ☐

- Have you talked to students about how they want to record their own
  learning? .... ☐

- Do your learning plans take account of:

  reinforcement of learning? .... ☐

  generalisation of skills? .... ☐

Resources

The ALBSU Standards for Basic Skills Teachers, (1992, ALBSU).

A New Life: Transition learning programmes for people with severe learning difficulties who are moving from long-stay hospitals into the community, (1992, Further Education Unit).

Primarily aimed at people working with adults with learning difficulties moving from long stay hospitals back to the community. This pack contains useful guidance on self assessment and assessment for all adults with learning difficulties.

Changing Relationships: Shared Action Planning, Ann Brechin & John Swain, (1987, Harper & Row).

CHAPTER 3

Selecting learning materials

What materials help people to learn?

People need to be interested in order to learn. Students will be more motivated if materials are:

- **RELEVANT** to their experience and lives.

- **REAL LIFE** rather than simulated.

- **ADULT** to reflect their adult status.

What does this mean in practice?

In	*Out*
Real money	Plastic money. Coin stamps
Clocks & watches	Cardboard clocks
Adult reading books	Children's books such as the Ladybird series
Real objects for colour recognition and counting such as pencils	Plastic cotton reels, building blocks and other pre-school materials
Newspapers, leaflets and magazines	Children's comics
Writing a letter for a real life purpose	Writing a letter that will never be posted
Making a telephone call for a reason	Practising on pretend phones that aren't connected

Teenage interests

You may find that some students are addicted to TV programmes and pop stars popular with teenagers – from Grange Hill and Byker Grove to Jason Donovan and Take That. These passions should be respected and can provide a useful basis for basic skills work, for example from studying the TV Times to reading record titles and lyrics.

> Helen is an outgoing woman in her thirties. She is very involved in the self advocacy movement, and has been taken part in a number of major conferences. She has a responsible job which involves working to represent the interests of people with learning difficulties in her area. She reads a great deal and enjoys young teenage fiction. She also loves Kylie Minogue and Neighbours.

How could you as a tutor build on Helen's existing interests, but also introduce her to more adult reading materials?

All learning activities should be meaningful to the student, and should have a clear purpose related to the student's goals. The materials you use will, of course, depend on the learning you are planning. The following is a rough guide to some of the materials and equipment that could be used.

Practical hints

- Ask around to see what is available locally before you rush to make or buy things.
- Ask if there is a resources budget which you can draw on.

An overview of learning materials

- The ALBSU publication *'Resources: A guide to material in adult literacy and basic skills'*, provides an invaluable source book.
- Material from other courses the student is taking.
- Materials of specific interest to individual students based on personal learning goals.
- Photocopier.
- Basic stationery – pens, pencils, paper, cardboard, folders.
- Leaflets.

44

- Flash cards e.g. of social sight words.
- Brochures.
- Labels from jars, tins, packets and medicines.
- Magazines.
- Newspapers.
- Books.
- Worksheets – commercially produced, borrowed or home made.
- Photographs – purchased, or produced by tutor and/or students.
- Cameras (Polaroids are good for quick feedback).
- Videos/video recorders/video cameras.
- TV.
- Overhead projector and screen.
- Tape recorders.
- Blank tapes for recording voices and interviews.
- Pre-recorded tapes – of books, sounds or music.
- Records/record player.
- Slides/slide projector.
- Games – adult rather than childish.
- Puzzles such as crosswords and word searches.
- Calculators.
- Computers, software and concept keyboards.
- Typewriters.
- Money – coins & notes.
- Watches & clocks.
- Learning packs on different subjects such as self advocacy or spelling.
- Access to facilities for particular group projects – perhaps developing photos/producing a newsletter/growing tomatoes/baking a cake etc; all of which could be used as a springboard for developing basic skills.

- Access to a laminating machine or to laminating film is useful. If you have spent a lot of time making a game or flashcards, you'll want to keep them looking good for as long as possible.

Materials on rights, self advocacy and other issues of interest written for adults with learning difficulties

Some materials have been produced particularly for people with learning difficulties in order to explain rights, self advocacy and other issues of interest in an easy to understand format. There is certainly scope for drawing on these materials in the context of basic skills work, where it is of relevance. These include:

- *Residents' Rights*, which explains what rights you have in your own home.

- *Oi, It's My Assessment*, from People First.

- A video about self advocacy made by people with learning difficulties in Walsall.

- Packs on self advocacy from Skills for People and Values Into Action.

The Norah Fry Research Centre at the University of Bristol has a policy of producing research in a format which is accessible for adults with learning difficulties. Large print, clear language and illustrations help to make the text readable. There are recent publications on people with learning difficulties as victims of crime and on a study of self advocacy groups. Forthcoming titles will address citizen advocacy and complaints procedures for adults with learning difficulties. Further details of all these materials are given at the end of this chapter.

Many social services departments, health service providers and voluntary organisations are starting to produce material in a form intended for adults with learning difficulties. For example, service charters or information about complaints procedures may be available in an accessible format in your area.

Community facilities

Community based facilities and activities can be used as a resource in developing learning programmes, for example:

- Using the library.

- Visiting museums and art galleries.

- Going shopping.

- Using pubs, coffee bars and restaurants.

- Planning a day out.

- Using public transport.

- Visits to the fire station, or police station.

- Going to parks and gardens.

- Trips to the theatre or cinema.

- Social events such as meals out, dances, parties.

- Using the leisure centre.

In South Glamorgan, adults with learning difficulties have visited a brewery and a cathedral as part of their studies.

A word of warning

Visits must have a clear educational rationale of which the basic skills elements must be an integral part. A trip out can provide students with the chance to practise making arrangements, using public transport, using money etc. However, there is a danger of adults with learning difficulties becoming "eternal day trippers" if trips out are not planned appropriately and without a clear purpose.

Adapting and making materials

It is quite likely that you will have to adapt or make materials and resources to suit the particular needs of your students. Here are a few things to think about:

- Are materials clear and unambiguous?

- Are the steps involved in any learning activity broken into small stages? Is this reflected in the materials?

- Is the language easy to understand? You may want to simplify the text if long or complicated words are used. See the ALBSU leaflet "*Making Reading Easier*".

- Is the type on any printed materials a suitable size? Beginning readers and people with a degree of visual impairment often find large type easier.

Options include:

- Blowing up print on a photocopier that enlarges

- Using a word processing package with a choice of fonts.

You will want material that uses some of the student's personal language, and you will inevitably have to make this yourself. You will find that some commercially produced packs and worksheets:

- will not start at a basic enough level

- will not have the stages broken down into small enough steps

- may have childish illustrations, if they are not specifically for adults.

Sharing ideas

There may already be a bank of worksheets and materials produced by tutors held centrally in your area. Ask around and find out.

Working together with other tutors can be productive and mutually useful:

- One team of three tutors working with adults with learning difficulties have developed three A4 ring binders, filled with master copies of worksheets they have produced on everything from shopping to cooking. They can photocopy worksheets from the files.

- One county has developed a magazine of materials made by part time tutors, which is widely circulated. The materials focus particularly on adults with severe learning difficulties.

Making and adapting materials – practical hints

- Think carefully about what you are making and why

- Make sure it's not available locally – you may be re-inventing the wheel!

- Keep it simple

- Use large type or print clearly

- Don't crowd the page

- Use pictures to help beginning readers (pictures can be begged, borrowed or done yourself – as long as they don't look childish).

Finding appropriate images and symbols can be difficult and time consuming. One possible source that some people have found useful is 'clip-art' – computer graphics designed for 'pasting' into documents produced by a word processor or desk-top publishing software. Although intended mainly for business, the images can often be adapted for other purposes. In addition, less commercially oriented collections are becoming increasingly available. The advertising pages of the main personal computer magazines are a good source of information, although care needs to be taken to ensure that any product is compatible with the software and hardware you are using.

Using computers

Computers are increasingly available, and some of your students may have their own at home. Find out if there is one or more available for you to use in your class, and ask for help if you are new to using them. The ALBSU *Basic Skills Software Guide* provides details of suitable programmes. Here are some examples of ways in which computers can be used:

- For students with limited co-ordination, a concept keyboard overlay simplifies the computer's own keyboard. Single words, letters or pictures can be bought or made to suit an individual's needs.

- Students can learn to load programmes and use them. Commercially available programmes include many basic skills ones – from telling the time to a computerised version of the spelling game "Hangman".

- Students can learn to word process. A "Spellcheck" facility can help to correct spellings. If students have poor hand writing, the word processor offers an adult and legible way of writing. Different fonts mean that various sizes and styles of print are available. Larger print suits beginning readers and those with a visual impairment.

- Student writing generally looks better when it is word processed. Some packages enable you to run a newspaper format, which is great for newsletters and magazines. One group wrote poems, which were word processed and then printed on marbled paper for a really special effect.

Computer assisted learning for people with learning difficulties has been with us for some time; computer programmes for teaching numeracy in particular are commonplace. Many people with learning difficulties have well developed 'television watching' skills, and will focus on a computer longer than they would in other contexts. The British Institute For Learning Difficulties (BILD – formerly BIMH) provide a reading list on the subject (see page 24 for BILD's address).

However, the development of 'multi-media' computing offers potential opportunities for people with learning difficulties that have yet to be tapped. The term multi-media refers to the combination of high quality sound and moving video images with conventional computer programmes. It is now possible to take the traditional book format and make it literally come alive on a computer screen. Unlike conventional videos where the viewer plays an essentially passive role, multi-media programmes can be interactive; the 'reader' can explore the text, following their own lines of interest.

The potential power of multi-media has already been recognised in higher education. Yet paradoxically it perhaps has most to offer people for whom conventional books are of limited value. The ability to 'voice over' text, coupled with the immediacy of animated or video footage, makes multi-media an ideal format for people who are not strong readers, both in terms of an individualised learning tool, and as a way of conveying information. However, despite the huge drop in costs over the last year, multi-media equipment is still going to be considerably more expensive than the cheap micro computers now in use in many day centres or colleges. There is a danger that the people who have most to gain from the information revolution may be the last to get access to it.

Task sheet

► Look through existing resources for the following materials:

- Readers for beginners

- Learning about maps

- Help with spelling words related to travel, such as bus stop, station and tickets.

► Which of the materials you find can be used as they stand?

► How would you use them?

► What supplementary materials, such as worksheets or flashcards, would you need to make for your students?

► How could you use or adapt the following:

- A supermarket leaflet on healthy eating

- A leaflet on how to open a building society account.

► Look at some of the catalogues or leaflets from the suppliers listed at the end of this chapter.

► Decide what is useful and what is not, based on the pictures and the information given.

Checklist

- Have you checked what materials are already available locally – both commercially produced and made by other tutors? .... ☐
- Have you checked whether you have a resources budget available? .... ☐
- Have you thought about how and where you will store materials that you have bought, borrowed or made? .... ☐
- Have you thought of ways in which adults with learning difficulties can find learning materials for themselves? .... ☐

References/resources

Resources: a guide to material in adult literacy and basic skills, (1986; updated 1992, ALBSU).

Basic Skills Software Guide, ILECC (1992, ALBSU).

Making Reading Easier, ALBSU information leaflet.

Making Reading "Easier", Mary McGarva (Spring 1989, ALBSU Newsletter Insert).

1001 Pictures for Teachers To Copy, Andrew Wright (1984, Collins).

Read Easy: Reading resources for adults with learning difficulties, Margaret Marshall & Dorothy Porter (1990, Whitakers).

This directory includes details of books, audio visual materials, games and computer software.

Materials for people with learning difficulties on rights, self advocacy and other issues

For Ourselves. Video made by Walsall self advocacy group. Details from Learning for Living, Whitehall School, Weston Street, Walsall, WS1 4BQ.

Residents' Rights: Helping people with learning difficulties understand their housing rights, P. Allen and C. Scales (1990, Pavilion Publishing).

Speaking Up for Yourself: How to plan and run courses that really help, Skills for People, Haldane House, Tankerville Terrace, Newcastle upon Tyne, NE2 3AH.

Oi! It's My Assessment, People First, Instrument House, 207-215, King's Cross Road, London WC1X 7DB.

Speaking Up for Yourself, Ken Simons (1993, Norah Fry Research Centre, 3, Priory Road, Bristol BS8 1TX).

Crime against People with Learning Difficulties, Dr Christopher Williams (1993, Norah Fry Research Centre, as above).

Learning About Self Advocacy, (1988, Values Into Action, Oxford House, Derbyshire Street, London E2 6HG).

Suppliers of learning materials

N.B. Some general educational suppliers have school materials in catalogues. Care must be taken to sift out adult and age appropriate products.

Adult Literacy & Basic Skills Unit (ALBSU)
Commonwealth House
1-19 New Oxford Street
London WC1A 1NU
Tel: 071-405 4017.

ALBSU publishes adult literacy and numeracy materials. Some materials are appropriate for use with adults who have learning difficulties, while others can be adapted.

E.J. Arnold
Parkside Lane
Dewsbury Road
Leeds LS11 5TD
Tel: 0532 772112

Avanti Books
1 Wellington Road
Stevenage
Herts SG2 9HR
Tel: 0438 350155/741131

Avanti stocks teaching packs, games, books and computer software. A postal service is available.

Games Galore
c/o Jane Gillard
53 Sunnyvale Drive
Longwell Green
Bristol

Games designed and produced by WEA students with learning difficulties.

Nordis Industries
Cornhill Close
Lodge Farm Industrial Estate
Northampton NN5 7UB
Tel: 0604 754358

Nordis produces educational computer software for adults with learning difficulties.

Living and Learning
Duke Street
Wisbech
Cambs PE13 2AE
Tel: 0945 63441

Resources for Learning Difficulties
(The Consortium)
Professional Support Centre
Beaufort House
Lillie Road
London SW6 1UF
Tel: 071-610 3755

Taskmaster Limited
Morris Road
Leicester LE2 6BR
Tel: 0533 704286

Winslow Press
Telford Road
Bicester
Oxon OX6 OTS
Tel: 0869 244644

Winslow Press have a range of products to include materials for developing life skills and photographs for language work.

Computer aided learning

Information is available from:

Peter Fowler
National Council for Education Technology
Unit 6
Science Park
Sir William Lyons Road
University of Warwick
Coventry CV4 7EZ

CHAPTER 4

Learning in action

This chapter offers a summary of the different ways of teaching skills. It also looks at what can go wrong – questions to consider when a student is failing to make progress. Lastly, it offers an overview of factors which can complicate learning: communication difficulties, physical or sensory impairments.

By the time you actually begin teaching, you will have:

- encouraged the student to assess his or her own learning needs

- decided, preferably together, on objectives

- chosen learning materials

- planned how you are going to teach something.

Strategies for teaching

This section below offers some tried and tested approaches to teaching. However, there is no one "right" way to teach something to a student, although as you will find out, there are plenty of ways that don't work! We all learn in different ways. You may have to try a number of different methods until you find one that works for a particular student. You will find specific suggestions for teaching literacy, numeracy and communication in the next chapter.

Demonstration

If you are teaching a physical skill – such as using a tin opener or folding a letter to put in an envelope – you will inevitably find it much easier to show someone how to do this, rather than simply telling him or her. You can, of course explain at the same time, in simple language.

Physical prompt

With learning a new skill that requires physical co-ordination, such as using a vending machine or holding a pen, it may help to guide the student's hand or arm at the initial stages. A physical prompt can gradually be reduced to a gestural prompt and then down to a verbal prompt.

Gestural prompt

A gestural prompt – such as indicating where to put the money in a vending machine – can remind students of the task.

Verbal prompt

A verbal prompt is a spoken reminder e.g. "Where are you going to put the money in the machine?"

Fading

Prompts can gradually be reduced until the student can perform the task alone. The process of gradually withdrawing the cues is called "fading" or "extinction".

Backward chaining

It is sometimes helpful to break tasks down (see the description of task analysis on page 29 Chapter 2), and then to teach the last part first. For instance, in the vending machine example, you may want to teach in the following stages:

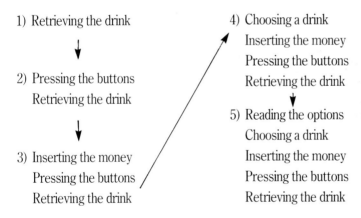

1) Retrieving the drink

2) Pressing the buttons
   Retrieving the drink

3) Inserting the money
   Pressing the buttons
   Retrieving the drink

4) Choosing a drink
   Inserting the money
   Pressing the buttons
   Retrieving the drink

5) Reading the options
   Choosing a drink
   Inserting the money
   Pressing the buttons
   Retrieving the drink

Motivation/reward

In this example, the motivation or reward of a drink is always a feature of the learning programme in question.

Sometimes the pleasure of learning a new skill will be rewarding in itself. At other times, people will respond positively to verbal encouragement or praise from the tutor if they have done well.

"That's great", "Well done" or similar phrases are often enough to make a student feel good about a piece of successful learning. Remember students are adult and **never** refer to them as "good boy" or "good girl".

When you're teaching – practical hints

- *Have everything ready before the session begins.*
- *Use simple, clear language. It's easy to use jargon or long words!*
- *Be flexible – you may have to alter your plans as you go along.*

Thinking on your feet

You may have to revise things as you go along. The task you have set your student may be too hard or too easy, in which case you will have to adjust the session accordingly.

Responding to the "now" factor

You may find that, for various reasons, you have to revise what you had planned to do. For example, perhaps some students are away because they are ill or the transport has broken down, which affects your planning for individuals or groups.

Seizing the moment

On the other hand, perhaps you have carefully planned a literacy session. Your student arrives with a new watch, desperate to learn to tell the time. Ignoring this urge would be a missed opportunity to capitalise on the student's motivation and enthusiasm. You will have re-schedule your planned work for another session.

When learning isn't taking place

Sometimes, despite careful planning and teaching, the student fails to learn. Here are some factors to consider:

- Have you broken the task down into small enough steps?
- Have you built in revision of the previous stages of learning?
- Has the student reached a plateau in his or her learning?
- Is the student bored or lacking in motivation?
- Is the student tired or drowsy?

Some people may be on medication which impairs their concentration and retention of learning. Epileptic fits may also temporarily "undo" learning.

If the student is not learning, it is your responsibility to revise and reconsider different approaches and strategies which can be tried. Occasionally nothing will work – as with Clive (see page 7), who really wanted to learn woodwork and not basic skills – and both tutor and student will need to reappraise the entire situation.

Factors which can complicate learning: communication difficulties, physical or sensory impairments

Learning can be made more difficult if students with learning difficulties also have communication problems and/or additional physical or sensory impairments. The adaptations you may need to make to your teaching are so individual, that to consider all possible permutations is beyond the scope of this book. However, as a starting point, a brief overview and useful addresses are given for various aspects of communication difficulties, sensory and physical disabilities.

Teaching students with communication difficulties

A number of adults with learning difficulties have difficulty in communicating clearly. Some students have mild speech impediments which you will probably find you "tune into" as you get to know them.

Some students may be shy or withdrawn and only speak when they feel relaxed or confident enough:

> Martin came to the NIACE / Lancaster University Summer School. He was very quiet and did not speak. One of the co-ordinating tutors assumed he had little or no language, and started using Makaton with him. Martin indicated that he wanted to use the 'phone. The tutor was most surprised when Martin loudly declared "I've got a new keyworker!" to his friend on the other end of the telephone . . .

Other students may use particular methods or communication aids to support their speech, such as those outlined below. Speech therapists working locally with adults with learning difficulties may be able to offer advice and training. Relevant addresses are also given in the resources section of this chapter.

Makaton: a signing system

Makaton is a signing system which is a modified version of British Sign Language. You need to go on a course to learn Makaton correctly. Makaton symbols are also available, to back up the signs.

57

Blissymbols: a symbol based communication system

Bliss is a symbol based communication method. Small pictures and symbols are laid out on a communication board, and symbols can be pointed to.

Examples of communication aids

Communication aids can be very costly, and need careful matching to the person's skills and physical abilities. Speech therapists can advise on their suitability and availability.

My Voice uses symbols in connection with a concept keyboard. When the symbols are pressed, a tape recorded voice message is activated.

The *Canon Communicator* can be used by people who can read and write to basic level or above, but who cannot speak clearly. Words and messages are typed into the machine, and emerge on a thin band of paper.

Facilitated communication

Facilitated communication is a method by which a key board or letter board is used by someone with communication problems, with physical support from an enabler. This support may vary from an encouraging hand on the shoulder through to shaping of the hand to enable an index finger to be pointed. The Community Options Facilitated Communication Project was set up in 1992 to introduce this approach to Britain (see resources listing for address). Facilitated communication is controversial. Some professionals are strongly opposed to it and are convinced that the facilitators end up 'leading' the person. Equally, there are supporters who claim to have witnessed dramatic developments in the communication skills of individuals using this method. Facilitated communication would appear to be an option worth exploring for some adults with learning difficulties, but it is worth bearing in mind that there well may be opposition from some professionals.

Teaching students with a visual impairment

Some students with learning difficulties may have slipped through the net when it comes to having their sight checked. Undiagnosed cataracts and other eye defects are considered to be a major problem for adults with learning difficulties. It is worth finding out:

- Have your students had their sight tested recently?

- Do any of them wear glasses (or have glasses at home?) for close work? – If so, can they bring them to classes?

If students have impaired vision or no sight, the Royal National Institute for the Blind (RNIB) is a useful source of leaflets, advice, information and aids. They produce a journal called *Focus*, which is a newsletter for staff working with people with visual and learning disabilities. The Focus factsheets series include one on hints for teaching skills to blind people with learning difficulties, and one on sight testing adults with learning difficulties.

Teaching students who are deaf or hard of hearing

Specialist tuition or support from a trained communicator will be needed for deaf students with learning difficulties who use British Sign Language.

For students who are partially deaf or hard of hearing, consider:

- Does he/she use (or have) a hearing aid?

- Is it turned on and correctly adjusted?

For students who have acquired a hearing loss, learning to lip read may help them. Remember if someone lip reads, you must speak clearly, face the person and remember not to cover your mouth with your hands.

A practical guide to teaching deaf adults entitled *Education and Deaf and Hard of Hearing Adults* is produced by NIACE.

Teaching students with physical disabilities

Some adults with learning difficulties have limited physical mobility and some use wheelchairs. Pointers to think about include:

- physical access to the teaching area

- physical access to other areas such as the toilets, canteen/cafeteria, and library

- physical access for any trips out planned, to include transport that is wheelchair accessible if necessary

- any aids or adaptations that might be needed, such as extra thick pens/pencils that are easier to grasp, or a concept keyboard, which simplifies the use of a computer.

Teaching students with multiple disabilities

It is possible that a student with learning difficulties may have a combination of disabilities. This does not mean that he or she cannot effectively participate in a basic skills group, as the following example shows:

Derek lives in a long stay hospital for people with learning difficulties. He attends adult education classes on site, run by the local college. Derek uses a wheelchair to get about. He has very poor eyesight, and can just about make out letter shapes. He has dictated his life story, and put it on tape. He has also made excellent progress in a communication and self advocacy group. His manual dexterity is poor, and he can barely trace his name written in large letters. However, he is starting to make progress with his reading using a large magnifying glass, and is also keen to experiment with the recently acquired computer.

Task sheet

1) Put a tape recorder in the corner of the classroom, switch it on and leave it recording.

   Later, listen to the tape and consider:

   ▶ Who is speaking most? Is it you?

   ▶ Are you dominating the group and always taking the lead, or are students playing an active role?

   ▶ Is your language clear and accessible?

2) Find out more about sign and symbol systems which can be used by adults with learning difficulties, such as Makaton and Blissymbols. Do any of your students use these methods of communication?

Useful books are:

▶ *Sign and Symbol Communication for Mentally Handicapped People* by Philip Jones and Ailsa Cregan (Croon Helm, 1986).

▶ *Signs and Symbols* by Chris Kiernan, Barbara Reid and Linda Jones (1983, Heinemann).

Checklist

- Have you assessed by informal observation your students':

  - physical mobility? .... ☐
  - manual dexterity? .... ☐
  - eyesight? .... ☐
  - hearing? .... ☐
  - communication skills? .... ☐

- Have you prepared back up activities as an emergency contingent in case your planned activities fall through – for example if some students are ill or transport breaks down? .... ☐

- Have you a summary of learning activities available so that in case you are ill, another tutor can step into the breach? .... ☐

Resources

Makaton

Information from:
The Makaton Vocabulary Development Project
31 Firwood Drive
Camberley
Surrey

Blissymbols

Information from:
The Blissymbolics Communication Resource Centre (UK)
Thomas House South Glamorgan Institute of Higher Education
Cyncoed Centre
Cynoed Road
Cardiff CF2 6XD
Tel: 0222 757826

Certain Bliss materials are available from:
Winslow Press
Telford Road
Bicester
Oxon OX6 0TS

Information and Practice Development Service on Multiple Disability
Royal National Institute for the Blind
224 Great Portland Street
London W1N 6AA
Tel: 071 388 1266

The Community Options Facilitated Communication Project
72 Northend
Batheaston
Bath BA1 7ES

References

Education and Deaf and Hard of Hearing Adults, Lesley Jones in Association with NIACE (1993 NIACE).

CHAPTER 5

Getting started – ideas for communication, literacy and numeracy

This chapter offers a starting point for ideas for teaching communication, literacy and numeracy. It is a menu of ideas and approaches from which you can:

- pick selectively to meet the needs of your students
- take an idea, expand and adapt it to suit your particular purposes.

Purposes of basic skills tuition

Each student will bring his or her own and highly individual goals to the learning situation. However, there are a number of important background purposes in teaching basic skills which we as tutors need to bear in mind when we are planning. Before looking at specific ideas for teaching, let us look at some of the reasons why what we are doing is important.

Basic skills is about developing confidence

Feeling better about being able to speak up, add up or read new words raises levels of confidence and self esteem. We as tutors should be thinking all the time about how we can raise our students' levels of confidence in different situations.

Basic skills is about developing competence

Students want to acquire new skills. It is our role to actively plan our teaching so that people are learning in the most effective way.

Basic skills is about fostering independence

Giving people greater independence through developing their basic skills is essential. Whether we are enabling someone to catch a bus alone for the first time, to go shopping without help, or to pay their own bills, enhancing personal independence should underpin everything we teach. This is sometimes particularly challenging where students are passive or institutionalised.

Basic skills is about developing a voice for students

Basic skills offers a vital avenue for students to express themselves, to develop their identity and self image. Talking and writing about their lives is one way of validating the experiences of students. This aspect is especially crucial because adults with learning difficulties can often have a poor self image due to not being listened to or taken seriously. There is a role for life story work, newsletters, magazines, poetry and reminiscence work, as long as it is part of an overall strategy.

Basic skills must support other areas of people's lives

Adults with learning difficulties who are on horticulture courses or working in shops, factories or cafes need to learn basic skills relevant to their particular needs. The same goes for the man moving out of a hostel to live in his own flat, or the newly wed couple who need to learn how to cook for themselves. All the time we must be thinking about how what goes on in the teaching situation relates to people's real lives.

Offering a range of choices

A wide range of topics can encompass different aspects of literacy, numeracy and communication. One day centre has a choices board, with topics that students can select from. These topics are changed regularly. On one occasion the centre was visited, the choices included the following:

- Bus training
- Discussion group
- Signs and symbols
- World religions
- Tuck shop
- Fun quiz
- Health and beauty
- Elvis
- Famous composers
- Darts in the pub
- Making poems
- Czech Republic.

Task

Think how you could use some of the above topics as a springboard for work on basic skills. How can you build choice into the basic skills curriculum for adults with learning difficulties?

Ideas for communication

Why communication?

Developing confidence in speaking and listening is a fundamental part of basic skills.

64

Communication helps us amongst other things:

- to relate to other people
- to express choices, views and opinions
- to tell other people what we want or need
- to give or follow directions or instructions.

Group discussion can provide a role for stimulating language development as well as offering a potential basis for related literacy and numeracy work. Oral skills form part of the Wordpower course and certificate.

English for Speakers of Other Languages (ESOL) classes may be available in your area for students with learning difficulties whose first language is not English. Some students with learning difficulties attend ESOL classes with relatives or on their own, while one or two areas have ESOL classes just for adults with learning difficulties.

Discussion topics/themes – an ideas list from students

Topics for discussion are best generated by the students involved. Groups of adults with learning difficulties have chosen to discuss the subjects below at various times. Ask your students what they would be interested to talk about – but also have ideas of your own for them to choose from in case of need.

- Current affairs
- Hobbies/interests
- Where I live
- Where I work
- Choices I make

- Friends
- Families
- Wages in day centres
- Holidays
- Vandalism.

- Public transport
- Planning a party
- Planning a day out
- Getting jobs

Ideas that tutors have used

Tape recorders

Tape recorders can be used by students to interview, for example:

- each other
- staff at the day centre or college

- celebrities
- MPs.

65

Recording an interview.

You will need:

blank cassette tape
tape recorder
microphone
list of questions
a quiet room

1. Remember to ask the person if they would like the interview to be taped. Some people do not like to be recorded on tape.

2. Decide where you and the person to be interviewed are going to sit. Place the microphone between you and the tape recorder where you can reach it.

3. Make sure the room is quiet and you are not going to be disturbed.

Sometimes the interviews have been turned into a magazine or newsletter article. See the resources section for details of an ALBSU article on using audio tapes in basic skills work. The worksheet opposite was designed by tutor Teresa Kirpilani using a computer.

Video

Using video is a good way to teach adults with learning difficulties about self awareness, and also stimulates language.

A day centre group had been meeting for several weeks to discuss their personal experiences of crime. When the group was filmed, the participants were very animated. One man described vividly how people he worked with at a farm had stubbed their cigarettes out on him, and how wrong he felt this was. He used language and vocabulary that the day centre staff had not heard him use before. As one member of staff exclaimed afterwards: "Where did he get those words from?"

Adults with learning difficulties have also successfully learnt to use video cameras in a number of places.

Photographs

Photographs can be used as the basis for language and discussion work, for instance:

- Making choices about lifestyles using photos (see resources list)
- Taking photos of each other with a Polaroid camera
- Taking photos of words around us.

Role play

Role play can help to prepare people for different situations, for instance:

- meeting new people
- talking to parents or staff and saying what you really want to
- buying a train ticket.

Videos/slides

Videos or slides from a range of sources can provide a stimulus for discussion.

Possibilities include:

- Self advocacy videos. Walsall LEA have produced one called *For Ourselves*.
- Health education videos and slides.

Music/sounds

Short pieces of music can be used to trigger discussion. Students can bring in their own favourite music to talk about.

Theme tunes from popular TV programmes recorded in snatches can also be used. What programme is it? Do you watch it? What do you think about it?

Libraries usually have records of interesting or unusual sounds which can be borrowed. Guessing what they are can be fun and practises listening skills. Sound lotto (where tape and picture or photo are matched) can be bought commercially or made at home.

Published materials which support the development of communication skills for adults with learning difficulties

Open University Course: Working Together – P555M

Working Together is the first Open University course aimed at adults with learning difficulties. It uses video, audio tapes and illustrated workbooks which cover a range of topics related to life issues – such as growing up and leaving home. The course is discussion based and can be studied by individuals with study partners, or by small groups. Students can obtain a certificate of course completion.

Learning about Self Advocacy: the LASA pack

The LASA pack goes through different stages of supporting adults with learning difficulties to speak up for themselves, including important points such as the differences between assertion and aggression, and the impact of body language.

Video First: ideas for using video in self advocacy

This book is aimed at adults with learning difficulties who want to use video to help them speak up. It is well laid out with large print and illustrations.

Ideas for Literacy

Readers may wish to supplement the information in this section by referring to the ALBSU publication '*An Introduction to Literacy Teaching*' compiled by Rose Gittins.

Writing

Observing your student writing

Adults with learning difficulties, like all basic skills students, will have different degrees of skill in writing. Observing what students can do already informs our teaching strategies.

A beginning writer: writing name and address

Questions to ask yourself:

- Can the student hold a pen or pencil comfortably?

- Can the student trace over or copy letters? (see name in dots as drawn in below).

- Can the student match his or her name or address to a base card when the words are cut up?

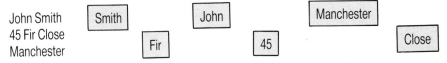

John Smith
45 Fir Close
Manchester

Has the student already been learning to write his or her name for the past 27 years? If so, is it really worth persisting? Is it a skill that will be used – e.g. to sign for money?

Would a card with personal details carried in a purse or wallet offer a shortcut?

An intermediate writer: writing notes, cards and lists

A personal spelling list or book can be used to help people record new words that they are learning to spell.

One method to help people remember new spellings is LOOK, COVER, WRITE, CHECK.

- You **look** hard at a word
- **Cover** it up
- **Write** it
- **Check** back to see how you did.

People may want to practice writing:

- greetings cards
- post cards
- shopping lists
- notes e.g. to order milk.

Envelopes.

You will need an envelope to send a letter in.

You will have to write the name and address of the person you are sending the letter to on the front.

Here is an example of an envelope addressed to Spike.

Spike Breakwell
99 Comedy Street
Luton
Beds.
LU3 634

Remember that you will need to buy a stamp to put on the envelope.

What is the cost of a first class stamp?

Where would you buy a stamp?

Filling in the missing words (known as cloze procedure) can help to develop both reading and writing skills. A cloze procedure on writing notes can be found on page 76/77. If they are notes and cards that will actually be sent, and lists that will be used, all the better. The Resources for Learning Difficulties Consortium produces pictorial shopping lists, which use pictures and words to help people who cannot recognise words alone. Labels can also be used from jars or packets to make a visual shopping list.

An advanced writer: writing letters and diaries

A student capable of writing a letter more or less independently may want to learn more about different sorts of letters, from informal ones to friends to formal ones enquiring about jobs. He or she may be interested to keep a diary, either during the class, in between sessions or both.

---

monday
On Monday I go to the club. I play billiards with numbers on them.

tuesday
On Tuesdays I watch T.V. I like watching Westerns.

wednesday
On Wednesdays I go out to the shops. I often buy coca cola, which I like very much.

Supporting people to do what they want

The above rough definitions do not mean, for instance, that a beginning writer could not tackle a letter. There are ways of getting round things:

- tracing over a tutor's writing (easy)
- copying under the tutor's writing (harder)
- copying from another page (harder still).

Alternatively, a letter could be sent by tape, or dictated. A letter sent for a purpose can have a real impact:

> Martin lived with his father, who died suddenly. Martin had not seen his brother, who lived 120 miles away, for 7 years. With the support of a basic skills tutor, he wrote to his brother. As a result, they met up and now see each other several times a year. Martin has successfully learnt to make the long journey, to include working out the coach fare and timetables.

Presentation

Students' work deserves to be presented in a valued way. The growing use of word processors has opened up great possibilities for students to learn basic word processing. For people with difficulty in handwriting, it may be easier to learn to use a keyboard than to write with a pen or pencil (see example opposite).

Creative ideas

Writing need not be confined to addresses and shopping lists. Student may like to write:

- Poetry
- Plays
- Stories.

They may be interested in producing:

- A newsletter or magazine
- A book
- A newspaper.

See Chapter 6 for examples of some ideas which have been developed.

Post Box

Dear Buzz,

This is a poster I did to put up at College.

> People First is a group of people - they speak up for themselves and say what they want.
> People with learning difficulties are also people, who have equal rights and shouldn't be called hurtful names - like 'handicapped' or 'a down's syndrome'. We should not be labelled differently. We all live the same life and breathe the same air.
> We are just the same - people like you, who have to live with what we are.
> We would like people to respect that instead of throwing abuse.
> We are just the same as you - we are still people.

Tazia Fawley

Dear Buzz,

I read the article about Graham Hamblett who works at Tescos. I work part time at Norah Fry, in the office. I do lots of different jobs. I've got a lot of friends who work here.
I have a timesheet. When I go home I fill it out for what time I've been here. I work from 2 O 'clock. Sometimes there's loads of letters and photocopying to do, but other times there's less. I also do shredding. I have to get the old paper ready for Friends of the earth to come and take the paper away to recycle.

I had an interview. They told me what the job was about, and asked me what I thought, and could I do the job? I said yes. I thought it went very well. I got a letter the next day saying I had the job.
I really enjoy the job. My cheque comes through in the post once a month. When some people leave, we sometimes go out for a meal to a posh restaurant.

Chris Brittain

5

My Life So Far

- Complete the sentences.

- Put the sentences in a sensible order.

1. I grew up in Luton I have always lived in Luton I do'nt Luton

2. very much but you have to put up with it.

My first memory is going on holiday mum and Dad to a farmhouse I liked watching the cows.

5. Now I like playing darts and goin to clubs and discas I go to Church.

4. I started school but I didnt like the first school very much The second school was very good

3. I wanted to sleep at night to make it easier for my mum when I was little I would like to take my mum to Australian if I could afford it.

74

Relating writing to vocational tasks

If students are on vocational courses, on work placements, or looking for work, there will be almost certainly be related writing tasks which they may want to work on during their basic skills sessions. These could include:

- Job application forms or letters
- Signing for a wage packet
- Filling in a time sheet
- Interview role play
- Looking for work in newspapers or at job centres.

A few areas have specialist job search teams, employed usually by Social Services to help adults with learning difficulties find and keep jobs, while all job centres have staff with a brief for disabled clients.

For people on specific courses or in particular jobs, writing tasks should be relevant to their needs. With permission from the student, liaison with the vocational tutor or employer can enable you as a tutor to plan learning that will directly benefit the student's basic skills at work. For example, this could include:

- writing labels for seed trays for horticultural students
- writing recipes for catering students
- listing stamps used or photocopies made for office work.

Independent living tasks

For students who are wanting to live more independently, writing tasks should be geared to their particular needs. Tasks might include:

- paying bills
- shopping lists
- signing for benefits
- signing bank or building society papers or books
- applying for a television licence
- filling in an electoral register form
- completing a form for a customer reading of a gas or electricity meter.

Notes

1) Dear Sarah

I am having a .... on holiday in .... because the weather is .... The beach is .... and .... The sea is .... I will be .... to come home.
With love, Linda

2) To the milkman.

Please leave two extra .... of .... today.
Thank ....

3) Dear Sir,

Please .... an application form for the post of .... I saw the advertisement in the ....
Yours .... S. Peters

4) Dear John,

Your dinner is in the .... I have gone to the .... I am feeling very .... today.
Love Sue

5) Dear Mrs Smith,

I am sorry the children are not at .... today. They are both .... with .... I hope they will be back .... week.
Best wishes, Clare Jones

6) Dear Aunt ....

Thank you very .... for the .... present. It is .... I will use it next time I .... a bath. I have always wanted a ....

....

Thanks again.

With love, from Sally

Reading

Beginning readers

Questions to ask yourself:

- Has the student's eyesight been checked recently? (A high proportion of adults with learning difficulties have undetected visual problems).

- Does he/she wears glasses? If so, can they be brought to all classes?

- Can the student recognise:
  - name?
  - address?
  - basic social signs? (see overleaf for a list).

Social sight vocabulary

Social signs are words we see around us every day.

They can be learnt:

- on flashcards, made by tutors or bought
- on photos, purchased or preferably taken locally out and about in the community
- out and about in real life contexts.

Some common social signs are shown on page 78. Be careful not to overwhelm students. It is best to start with a few selected signs that reflect the student's interests/ needs.

Ways to reinforce the learning of social signs can be devised and include:

- Bingo games (some are available commercially)
- Matching worksheets – matching the word to the sign
- Word hunts (See page 79).

Common Social Signs

BUS STOP	ON
CLOSED	OPEN
CROSS NOW	OUT
DANGER	PAY HERE
DOWN	POISON
ENGAGED	POLICE
ENQUIRIES	PRIVATE
ENTRANCE	PULL
EXIT	PUSH
GENTLEMEN	STATION
HOSPITAL	TELEPHONE
IN	TICKETS
KEEP OUT	TOILETS
LADIES	UP
LITTER	VACANT
MEN	WAIT
NO ENTRY	WAY IN
NO SMOKING	WAY OUT
OFF	WOMEN

Social Sight Word Hunt

```
T  O  I  L  E  T  S  B  A  P  Z  C  P
B  L  S  E  F  Q  R  T  L  U  G  Q  R
Z  M  P  C  L  A  D  I  E  S  E  D  V
Q  E  T  Y  S  L  J  V  O  H  N  S  R
R  N  O  B  M  L  P  W  Y  X  T  G  T
W  K  P  A  Y  H  E  R  E  A  L  N  H
I  Z  W  H  O  D  F  O  F  F  E  A  H
N  L  O  G  E  W  P  Z  R  G  M  S  B
D  J  M  R  X  K  L  O  U  T  E  L  M
O  N  N  S  T  V  P  U  L  L  N  O  H
```

TOILETS	IN
LADIES	MEN
PAY HERE	OFF
PUSH	OUT
GENTLEMEN	ON
PULL	

Where would you see these words?

If you can, write a sentence for each one saying where you would find it.

Language experience

Language experience is a term used for an approach which has proved helpful for beginning readers. See the resources listing for details of an ALBSU article on this subject.

- Talk with the learner about something which interests him or her.

- Write down what the student says.

- Be careful to use the student's words and language patterns – even if it doesn't sound grammatically correct.

- Use the text generated by the student to work on together to practice reading. One student wrote:

> *I worked down the farm with the chickens.*
> *It were hard but I liked it.*

The text can be read together. A copy can be made, and the words cut up to be matched to the original.

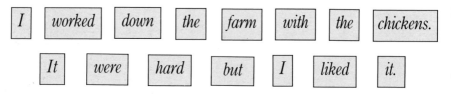

The students can gradually learn to recognise the words. Then new sentences can be made and read, for example:

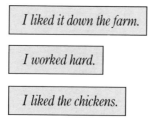

> *I liked it down the farm.*

> *I worked hard.*

> *I liked the chickens.*

Practical hint

> *A useful way of keeping cut up words and text tidy is to use a photo album to store them in.*

Developing reading skills further

Students will be keen to read about things that they are interested in. Ask people to bring in books, magazines or newspapers, and raid the local library with students. Joining the library in itself can be an education! Find out what resources are available from the local basic skills scheme. Here are just a few of the materials people have chosen to improve their reading:

- Pop magazines
- TV Times
- Horror stories
- Modern art books

- Cookery books
- Classic car magazines
- Football match reports
- Tourist information brochures.

There are a number of books written especially for adults who want to improve their reading. The publishers and suppliers listed in Chapter 3 stock these. One tutor describes how she uses published reading books as a springboard for making related materials to help with reading:

"I make my own worksheets to go with books. Students can choose the right word to complete a sentence, or fill the gap. I put some of the books on tape, so that people can listen to the story before they read it – or while they are reading it. Some of the books use a phonics approach which makes the text seem clumsy and awkward. "Pat put the pan on" – and so on. I've re-written and simplified the text of some readers."

Reading for meaning

Reading for meaning is important. Students will be more motivated to read material that is relevant and interesting to them. There is a debate about whether "look and say" – reading and recognising whole words – should be taught as opposed to phonics, where the emphasis is on letter sounds and patterns that are similar, as in "the cat sat on the mat". In fact, most people get by on a mixture of both approaches. Think how you would yourself sound out an unfamiliar word or nonsense word: phonics can give "word attack" skills. However, language experience begins with recognising whole words. There are advantages in reading for meaning. As one tutor of young adults with learning difficulties who used a phonics approach only commented: "They can read, but they can't understand what they're reading!"

Supporting reading skill development – practical hints

Make sure that whatever the student is learning to read is of interest to him or her.

Encourage anticipation of what is likely to be in the book. Ask the student to look for clues in the cover and any illustrations.

If a student reads a sentence and stumbles or pauses, prompt with the right word. You can go back and work on "hard" words later. Building confidence and fluency is more important than being word perfect.

Prepare the student as necessary by:

- *reading the text with the student*

- *putting the words on tape for the student to listen to. Speaking reasonably slowly makes it easier for the student to follow the text.*

How can you tell if the student is making sense of the text?

Simple comprehension questions about the content of the text can be helpful. This can be done orally, or in writing if the student is able. Other approaches include:

- choosing the right word (or phrase) to finish a sentence

- filling in gaps

- asking the student to tell you what the story or text is about in summary.

Critical reading

Particularly for adults with learning difficulties living independently, it is important to encourage them to question what they are reading when it comes to free offers, junk mail and special bargains. "FREE" written in large letters can be misleading.

Adults with learning difficulties are often capable of far more than we assume. Members of Advocacy in Action from Nottingham wrote a book review in cartoon format, which was published in an academic journal. They criticised the author for using the label "mental handicap".

Which word is right ?

1. In the hotel they had a nice (bar/~~bat~~)

2. We had breakfast in (~~bad~~/bed)

3. We (got/~~god~~) up and dressed.

4. The porters took our (~~dogs~~/bags) up.

5. I loaded the cases in the (car/~~can~~)

6. We (looked/booked) up in a hotel.

| Put the letters in the right order |

upb   rac   moor

agb   toob   rab

Following Instructions

RUM
Flavour Sauce Mix
JUST ADD BOILING WATER – NO ARTIFICIAL COLOURS OR PRESERVATIVES

DIRECTIONS

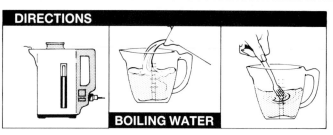

BOILING WATER

1. Put kettle on to BOIL.
2. Empty sachet into a measuring jug – add BOILING water to ¾ pint (425ml) level.
3. Whisk briskly with a fork until smooth and creamy.

INGREDIENTS

Sugar, Whey Powder, Modified Starch, Vegetable Oil (Hydrogenated), Dried Skimmed Milk, Caseinate, Flavourings.

NUTRITION

100g as packed provides:	A serving, prepared as instructed provides:	
Energy 1738kJ/ 410 kcal (calories);	Energy (calories)	80
Protein 6g;	Protein (g)	1.2
Carbohydrate 81g;	Carbohydrate (g)	1.8
Fat 9g.	Fat (g)	1.8

76g e

- Look at the food packet.

- What is the make of the sauce?

- What is kind of sauce is it?

- What must you add to make this sauce?

- How do you make the sauce?

- Would you use this sauce for a starter, main course or dessert?

Reading and work related tasks

As outlined in the section on writing, liaison with course tutors or employers (with student consent) can help to pinpoint exactly what skills people need to work on. Depending on the situation, you may find yourself teaching, for example:

- a student of horticulture how to read seed packets
- a factory worker to read safety warnings
- a supermarket shelf stacker to read labels on boxes in the warehouse
- a catering student to read lists of ingredients.

Reading and independent living tasks

Again, what is taught depends very much on individual circumstances, but students may want to learn to read materials such as those listed below:

- bus or train timetables
- recipes
- the TV Times
- food packets

- medicine labels
- what's on at the cinema
- DIY instructions.

Ideas for numeracy

"People don't realise how far back you've got to go. There's a gulf of understanding. The college referred somebody to learn to work out change. She hasn't got much number concept, and can't count to five . . ."

Starting with basics

Counting with meaning and relating each number to an object (called "one to one correspondence") is the starting point for getting a grasp on numbers.

Sometimes adults with learning difficulties will have been taught to count by rote, but may not relate the words they are saying to objects. Hence people may recite "One - two - three - four - five" – when there are only two objects there. For basic counting, picking objects up and physically moving them as you say each number can encourage the link between the number and the object to be made.

Using numbers for a real purpose – e.g. putting out the right number of coffee cups and spoons – can help to reinforce basic counting.

Gaps

You may find that some people can count up to a certain fairly random point and then no further – perhaps 29 or 89! Teaching numbers beyond this point is then important. Number squares, with numbers written from 1 to 100, can be helpful for numbers within that range. Some people will be able to count orally, but not to write figures down. Other people will be competent and may be capable of doing quite advanced maths. It is possible to have someone struggling with counting to ten, and someone learning multiplication in the same group! It will be important to sort out the different levels in order to plan with students appropriately. See the check list at the back of this section for what to look out for in terms of students' capabilities in relation to money, time, number and measurement. You may find that retention of learning fluctuates. You may find for example, that a student will recognise a 50p coin one week and not the next. Consolidation and overlearning help the learning to be retained.

Numbers for real life

What numbers will be useful to the students in their real lives – and how can the link be made?

Yvette struggled in a basic skills class for ten years with literacy and numeracy, and made very little progress. The breakthrough came when she left to join a machine knitting class. Suddenly her numeracy developed in leaps and bounds as she learnt to count rows and stitches in order to pursue her interest. She also gained enough confidence to show another student how to use the machine.

Ideas for learning activities related to number

All of the activities outlined in this section relate to competencies described in the Numberpower course and certificate. In some cases, several competencies can be dealt within one topic.

Classroom games using coins and notes can be used to help familiarise people with matching and naming coins and notes. Bingo, dominoes, lotto and Monopoly have all been used in different versions by tutors. Money and shopping worksheets can offer back up activities on paper. However, there is a real danger that indoor classroom activities will not relate to real life and that learning will not be transferred. It is better, if possible, to use real life situations as the basis of developing work on money.

Many of the suggestions below involve going out into the community. This will obviously have implications for staffing and managing the group. An extra person to go out with one or two students, or to stay with the rest of the group, is essential. Talk to your co-ordinator or manager about whether it is possible to arrange for any of the following, for occasional trips out:

- a co-tutor to work with you for particular sessions

- a teaching assistant

- a volunteer (it is likely that references, training and a police check will be required)

- a member of staff from another agency. In one case, an adult education tutor and a community nurse ran a "shopping for lunch" group at a college

- a more able student to take less confident students out as a peer group tutor.

Buying a drink or snack at a cafe

- Deciding – is it self service or table service?

- Choosing what to have.

- Estimating the cost.

- Handing over an appropriate amount of money.

- Receiving change.

Some tutors have had success in persuading coffee bars and snack bars to let them have copies of menus (often illustrated) to help prepare students, and to do follow up work afterwards.

Buying tea or coffee and biscuits to have in the classroom or running a coffee bar for other students

Contributing a small amount of money each week for refreshments in class provides opportunities for:

- counting coins and notes

- making relevant purchases

- counting up numbers: who wants tea? Who wants coffee?

- getting the right numbers of mugs out.

Opening a building society account

One group opened its own building society account. Small amounts paid regularly by students covered refreshments and a termly outing. People learnt about:

- filling in the relevant forms
- writing and signing cheques
- paying in and withdrawing money.

Some building societies produce packs and games which tutors have found helpful, although in some cases they have needed to edit out any childish bits.

Working out bills

Students living independently may want support in working out bills for services such as rent, telephone, electricity, gas and water. There is scope for discussion about:

- How will you pay (Quarterly, weekly, budget account etc.)?
- How much will you need to put by?
- Are there ways to help you save up (e.g. phone stamps)?

Using a calculator

Using a calculator can be helpful in working out budgeting and shopping sums. If students have their own calculator at home, it makes sense for them to learn on that particular model.

Planning a day out

Planning a day out can provide a lot of scope for activities related to number:

- What do the various methods of transport cost? Compare train/bus fares.
- Which method is most convenient? Compare timetables.
- Are there any entrance fees, for instance to a museum or garden?
- What will be the cost of having a meal out compared to taking sandwiches?
- How much money will people need to bring?

Going shopping

Handling money when shopping beats sitting in a classroom with a worksheet. Asking for help if needed, queuing up and finding your way around a shop are all part of the process, which you can't effectively reproduce in a classroom! Tutors have used the following situations as learning activities:

- Buying a newspaper or magazine

- Buying toiletries to go on holiday

- Shopping for food to cook for lunch

- Buying swimming tickets at the leisure centre

- Buying a birthday card.

Observing students when shopping will also give you clues about how they currently deal with situations:

Pat regularly bought small items. He always handed over a £1 coin. This strategy worked well – except that he subsequently ended up with pockets full of change which he didn't feel confident to use.

Richard spent years in a long stay hospital. He had worked out that bronze coins were of far less value than silver ones. His response on receiving change was to throw the 1p and 2p coins away.

Sheila could cope with going shopping with a list. However, when the tutor observed her discreetly, it became apparent that Sheila was buying the items in the precise order on the list. This meant going from one end of the shop to the other numerous times in search of the next item on the list. Shopping consequently took a very long time indeed!

Task

▶ What strategies could be developed to overcome these situations?

Have I Got Enough?

Which items can I buy with 50p?

45p

26p

COFFEE

21p

COCA COLA

30p

60p

After Dark Choc Mints

85p

- Find suitable coins to pay for each item.

- How much change should you get?

39p

TOMATO KETCHUP

12oz

I paid with _____

My change was _____

Fresh

BRITISH MINCED BEEF

78p PER LB

I paid with _____

My change was _____

NEW RAVE automatic

E3

82p I paid with _____

My change was _____

```
         ASDA CARDIFF
                                 .20
    TWIX                        1.69
    MINI KIEVS                  3.42
    ANDREX                      2.50
    MENS SOCK                   1.56
    ANDREX                       .78
    GRANNY SMITH                 .82
    APPLES                      3.75
    MENS SOCK                   1.99
    SINGLE                       .25
    ASSORTED                     .76
    ASSORTED                     .67
    BANANAS                      .99
    PENGUIN                     1.09
    SHREDDIES                    .99
    KP SKIPS                    2.39
    ASDA LASAGNE                 .11
    HUBBA BUBBA                  .87
    ASSORTED                     .28
    STRONG MINTS                 .47
    ST IVEL GOLD                2.09
    SV MOMENTS
                 SUB-TOTAL    27.67

    21   BALANCE DUE           27.67

                               28.00
         CASH                    .33
         CHANGE DUE

    02/10/91  16:56  8278  21     321

     THANK YOU FOR SHOPPING WITH US
```

Shopping

This is a till receipt from a well known supermarket.

Look at it carefully then answer the questions.

- Where were the goods bought?

- How many items were bought?

- What was the total of the bill?

- How was the bill paid?

- How much change was there?

- On what date were the goods bought?

- At what time of the day was I in the shop?

- Where was the store in which the items were bought?

Telling the time

Helping students to relate time to events is a way of helping them to make sense of months, weeks and hours.

Students can be encouraged to think about:

- what time they get up
- what time they go to bed
- what they do on particular days of the week
- what time and day favourite TV or radio programmes are on.

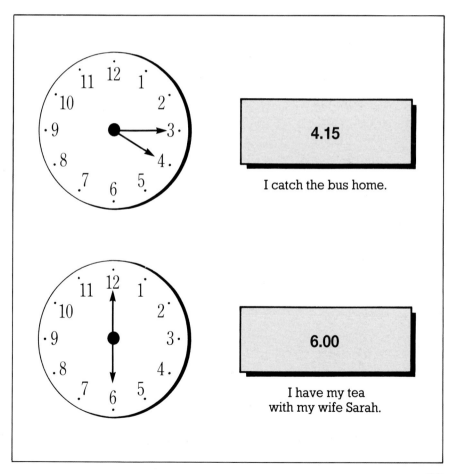

4.15

I catch the bus home.

6.00

I have my tea
with my wife Sarah.

93

Making a telephone call

Using a telephone requires number recognition and sequencing skills, as well as awareness of the different types of phone: is it a private phone, pay phone or card phone? How do you use it? What coins do you need? Where can you buy a phone card from? What do the different sounds mean? Anyone who has struggled to use a telephone in a foreign country will have some empathy with adults with learning difficulties trying to learn these things. Making a telephone call for a real purpose will be more meaningful for the student than making one for the sake of it. Taking photos of students making a telephone call can be useful to help recall the sequence of events.

Task

▶ Do a task analysis breakdown of all the steps involved in making a telephone call.

A checklist for number

This checklist for number is more detailed than the basic skills checklist for self assessment given in Chapter 2. It may help you and the students you are working with to pin-point more precisely what they want to focus on in terms of numeracy.

Money

1. I can sort coins by colour .... ☐
2. I can sort coins by size/shape .... ☐
3. I can name 1p, 2p .... ☐
4. I can name 5p, 10p, 20p .... ☐
5. I can name 50p, £1 coin .... ☐
6. I can name notes .... ☐
7. I can count in 10s, 5s, 2s .... ☐
8. I can count coins to 10p, 20p, 50p, £1 put together in different ways .... ☐
9. I know that 2 x 5p = 10p, 2 x 10p = 20p .... ☐

---

10. I can offer about the right money at the shops .... ☐

11. I can count out money to reach a specified amount .... ☐

12. I can work out change .... ☐

13. I can add up a shopping bill .... ☐

14. I can budget .... ☐

15. I can save at a bank or post office .... ☐

Time

a) Telling time

1. I can tell the time on the hour .... ☐

2. I can tell the time to ½ hour .... ☐

3. I can tell the time to ¼ hour .... ☐

4. I can tell the time exactly .... ☐

5. I can set a clock to a given time .... ☐

6. I can use 24 hour clock/timetable .... ☐

b) Concept of time

7. I understand before/after .... ☐

8. I know the days of the week .... ☐

9. I know what time things happen e.g. lunch at 1pm .... ☐

10. I know which day it is .... ☐

11. I know the months of the year .... ☐

12. I know which month it is .... ☐

13. I know the number of hours in a day .... ☐

14. I know the number of minutes in an hour .... ☐

15. I can plan events using a calendar or timetable .... ☐

16. I can work out how long things will take e.g. for cooking or making a journey .... ☐

Number

1. I can count up to 3 things ☐
2. I can count up to 5 things ☐
3. I can count up to 10 things ☐
4. I can put written numbers with the right number of things (up to 10) ☐
5. I can add to 10 ☐
6. I can count to 20 ☐
7. I can add to 20 ☐
8. I can subtract to 10 ☐
9. I can subtract to 20 ☐
10. I can count to 50 ☐
11. I can count to 100 ☐
12. I can write numbers to 50 ☐
13. I can write numbers to 100 ☐
14. I can add numbers involving carrying ☐
15. I can subtract double figures involving borrowing ☐
16. I can multiply using tables to 12 ☐
17. I can do long multiplication ☐
18. I can do short division ☐
19. I can do long division ☐

Measurement

1. I know the difference between big/little; tall/short ☐
2. I know the difference between heavy/light; full/empty ☐
3. I can measure things with a ruler or tape measure ☐
4. I know my own height and clothes size ☐

5. I can weigh things in kilos and grams or pounds and ounces .... ☐

6. I know my own weight .... ☐

7. I can weigh out a given weight .... ☐

8. I can measure liquids in pints or litres .... ☐

Task sheet

▶ Try out some of the ideas for developing communication skills.

How do they work in practice for your particular students?

Can you think of other ideas to try?

▶ Look at three different books for beginning readers.

How do they compare in terms of content and interest level?

Think about how you could make some simple worksheets to back up the text, and to help with revision and repetition of new words.

▶ Look at some of the suggested learning activities for numeracy.

How do they relate to the goals your students want to work on?

Think about making some materials for numeracy to cater for the needs of particular students in your group.

Checklist

● Have you made a list with students of possible topics for discussion?

● Do you understand how to use the following:
   – The language experience approach for beginning readers?
   – The "look, cover, write, check" approach for learning spellings?

● Have you worked out individual programmes for literacy and/or numeracy in consultation with students?

Resources for communication

"Lifestyles" photo pack from Pavilion Publishing (Brighton).

OU course *"Working Together"* (P555M) Details from:
The Open University
Walton Hall
Milton Keynes MK7 6AA
Tel: 0908 274066

The LASA Pack (See chapter 3 for details)

Details of Walsall *"For Ourselves"* self advocacy video
Learning for Living
Whitehall School
Weston Street
Walsall WS1 4BQ

Winslow Press have a good range of photographic materials (See chapter 3 for address).

Video First: ideas for using video for self advocacy (1993, Norah Fry Research Centre) (See Appendix for address).

Resources for Literacy

1000 pictures for teachers to copy, Andrew Wright (1984, Collins ELT).

An Introduction to Literacy Teaching, compiled by Rose Gittins (1993, ALBSU).

Making Reading "Easier", Mary McGarva (Spring 1989, ALBSU Newsletter Insert).

Using Audio Tapes in ABE, Nuala Govenden (ALBSU Newsletter No.41, Spring 1991).

Resources for numeracy

Henley College Maths Pack, Henley College, Coventry.

An Introduction to Numeracy Teaching, Jessica Brittan (1993, ALBSU).

The Numeracy Pack, Diana Coben and Sandy Black (1984, ALBSU; reprinted 1993).

CHAPTER 6

Developing themes and projects

This chapter looks at how you can build on the basic ideas in Chapter 5 to develop group work, themes and projects according to the interests and aspirations of the students involved.

Working as a group

Much of the work outlined in the previous chapter focuses on the individual. Some tutors divide teaching sessions and have individual work and group work in two separate slots divided by coffee. The strengths of group work are that:

- it enables discussion to take place, therefore promoting communication skills and interaction

- it allows themes or topics to be worked on and developed during one or more sessions

- more able students can take a role in peer tutoring students with fewer skills, e.g. helping out with spellings

- it promotes self advocacy and self determination when students are involved in choosing topics and options.

Group work requires careful planning so that individuals at different stages and levels can be fully involved. It is important to relate a group activity to individual achievements of competence. Factors to bear in mind when planning include the following:

- What stimulus material, if any, are you going to use? This could include pictures, photos, video, newspaper cuttings, magazines, text books, worksheets, etc.

- What is the relevance and purpose of the activity in relation to the students' learning? What objectives are you planning to be achieved?

- How will the group activity be evaluated by you and by the students?

Core themes for group work

Learning activities relating to **material from other courses** which students are taking. This could include, for example:

- work on sequencing photos or written instructions for practical skills such as woodwork, bricklaying, catering, horticulture or painting and decorating
- work on reading or spelling specific words in relation to a vocational course
- related numeracy tasks, whether weighing ingredients for catering or measuring for woodwork.

One scheme literally took basic skills into the potting shed:

> A college working with a horticultural project decided that the basic skills tutor would go "on site" and that the horticulture instructor would also come into college. A library was set up in the potting shed, with gardening magazines and books. Sending away for seed catalogues provided a real life purpose for practising basics like writing names and addresses, while the course content and requirements – from sowing leeks to planning a garden – gave considerable scope for related basic skills work.

- Work on **independent living tasks** which the group have a common interest in learning. This might range from work on using public transport or going to the cinema to shopping or form filling.

> One group decided to plan a weekend away to practise their skills for independence. They made travel arrangements and booked a hotel in Blackpool. Managing to cope away from home and practising their social skills in a real context helped the students to feel more confident.

- Developing **communication skills and confidence in speaking up** through group work. Shared experience can provide a powerful focus. In one area, a group of black women with learning difficulties met to talk about their lives. Photographs of positive images of black women provided valuable discussion material for one session. In another area, people talked with passion about their experiences as victims of crime. A newspaper cutting about a man with learning difficulties who had been attacked triggered the discussion.

Other activities can provide opportunities to practise specific skills in speaking and listening. These can range from developing the confidence to speak up in a group to assertiveness training or to role playing, for instance asking for help in a shop.

- Work based on **jobs or work experience** with learning goals that the group have in common. This could include topics on being punctual, getting on with people, filling in a time sheet and so on.

Ideas for group work topics involving a range of basic skills

Obviously the topics you choose will reflect the needs and interests of your students. The following ideas offer a few examples of the sorts of things that basic skills students have worked on in a group context:

- Arranging a trip out from start to finish, including making bookings, looking at travel options, working out costings and writing thank you letters if needed.

- Inviting speakers to visit and talk about something of general interest to the group. One group had a first aid talk and practical demonstration. There were lots of opportunities for related basic skills work – from reading medicine bottles to using easy to read thermometers.

- Healthy eating and menu planning. Health education materials, supermarket leaflets and food photographs can provide discussion material.

- Learning to vote. One group talked to local MPs and made a leaflet about how to vote just before elections took place.

- Bringing in items connected with hobbies or interests to share with other people and to talk and write about. In one group, individuals brought in a wide range of things – from embroidery and horror stories to country and western LPs.

- Compiling crosswords, word hunts or number/money games in twos or threes.

- Looking at holiday brochures, choosing where you would go and writing about holidays.

- Playing games to develop communication skills, such as the "What if?" game. Various scenarios are written on cards for students to respond to, such as:

  – "What would you do if you lost your purse?"

  – "What would you do if you won £100?"

Producing books about people's lives

Students may like to write or tape their own life story and illustrate it with photographs.

This piece of work:

- validates and values people's experiences
- allows for plenty of discussion

MICHELLE THOMAS' STORY

"I was always ill at school and slow at learning things . . .
they said I was unteachable . . .
that I couldn't be taught anything . . . that's why I had to leave.

They hadn't taught me things only these . . .
H is a "chair" . . . . .M is a "mountain".

"I never had a star at school. Everyone else did. It made me
feel I was no good – never be any good – useless. I was very
insecure – I tried – felt they didn't think anything of me.

A star means to children that they can achieve – work hard
at what you do to get anywhere. Without the star, children
think less of themselves. That's bad!

If I had my time over, I would tell them this:
'I've come a long way even though you taught me the wrong
things . . .'

I feel a bit bitter because if they had taught me properly then
I would have done more things with my life. By now I would
have gone on to do a lot more things . . .'

- enables oral, writing and reading skills to be developed. For example, it can produce a good piece of text to work on with the language experience approach (see Chapter 5).

The "Snapped Lives" project from the Rhondda combines words and photos to celebrate the lives of people with disabilities. An extract is shown on pages 102/103.

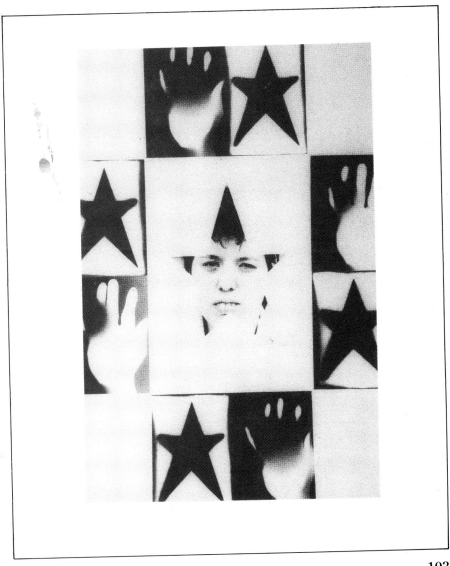

Reminiscence work

For groups of older adults with learning difficulties, thinking back to life as it used to be can provide much scope for discussion and tape recording and/or writing down memoirs.

Individual memories shared in a group

A group of older adults with learning difficulties in Bedfordshire met regularly to discuss the past. Their recollections were tape recorded and then written down, edited, and re-worked many times until the participants were satisfied with the results. Dorothy Atkinson from the Open University acted as a facilitator and has edited the resulting book, entitled 'Past Times'. Memories ranged from school days and the war to the trauma of being sent to live in a long stay hospital decades ago:

> 'When I was a little girl I was put away. I was 14 and a half. I went to Cell Barnes to live because they said I was backward. My dad refused to sign the papers for me to go, but the police came and said he would have to go to prison if he didn't. I cried when I had to go with the welfare officer.'

A collective experience remembered

In Bristol, the closure of Hortham Hospital resulted in groups of adults with learning difficulties moving back to live in the community.

A group of the former hospital residents chose to meet and talk about the hospital as it used to be, and the fact that their former home is now shut down.

The resulting discussions were written down, edited and illustrated. Their work has now been printed as "Hortham Memories" (see page 105 for an extract). The book provides reading material and offers a simplified version on the right hand page for beginning readers.

A word of warning

Thinking back can sometimes be painful. Bear this in mind – for example if a student has had an unhappy past he or she may prefer not to talk about it, or may need support to work things through. Remember though that you are an educator rather than a counsellor; the student may need professional help that you cannot offer to work through painful memories. A few students may have buried deep instances of:

- sexual abuse
- rejection
- unhappy childhood
- physical abuse.

Ask for help from your manager or co-ordinator if you are worried about a student.

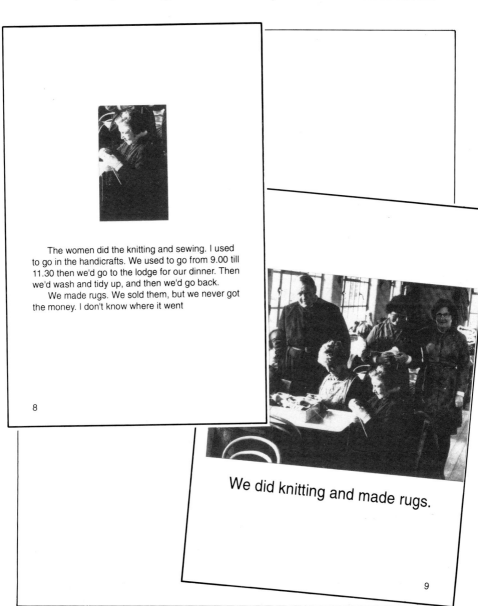

The women did the knitting and sewing. I used to go in the handicrafts. We used to go from 9.00 till 11.30 then we'd go to the lodge for our dinner. Then we'd wash and tidy up, and then we'd go back.

We made rugs. We sold them, but we never got the money. I don't know where it went

8

We did knitting and made rugs.

9

A magazine or newsletter

Collating student writing in the format of a magazine or newsletter can give students a clear goal to work towards. Some word processing packages offer an option for a newspaper style format to be produced.

Avon has a magazine called "Buzz", which is written by adults with learning difficulties, with support. It uses photos and large type to produce a lively, readable format (see page 107 for an extract). It is also available on tape.

"Buzz" has the advantage of being professionally produced and printed – but you can steal the ideas to try out locally with whatever resources you have available! "Buzz" is available by subscription – see the resources listing at the end of this chapter for details. For example, one group in South Glamorgan worked to produce the "Highfields Magazine". Students and tutors alike wrote for the magazine. David had been slowly learning the names of herbs to support his work on a herb garden project. His word hunt with the names of herbs in shown on page 108. Another word hunt was produced by Karen, who had done language experience work on bus drivers. The word hunt contained all the drivers' names. She also wrote about the bus drivers (see page 108). Jill (see also page 108) wrote about Highfields day centre. Other contributions included recipes, crosswords, jokes and poems.

Writing poetry: "We gets it out of our own heads"

When Avon People First (a self advocacy group) organised a conference in 1992 for other adults with learning difficulties, more participants chose the workshop on poetry, art and drama than all of the other options put together.

The Rushlands Poets meet every week to write new poems. Jane Sallis is the group worker, who has worked with the group since it was first established in 1988. Her advice is:

- let the ideas and words come from the students: "Don't ask leading questions – be subtle!"

- keep quiet when students are struggling for words: "It's tempting to step in, but better to be quiet".

- check back what people have said if they are dictating. "Ask – do you mean this word? Have I said it right?"

Out and About

Glastonbury

Glastonbury

Glastonbury is a very old town, with a museum, an Abbey, and a nice country walk to Glastonbury Tor. It has lots of different shops too.

You can get the 376 bus from Bristol bus station. It goes to Glastonbury every hour. It is on the A37 if you go by car.

The Abbey, the museu
year.

The Abbey costs £1 p
Glastonbury Tor is fre

If you are in a wheel
around. Glastonbury
There are two public
ing the roads in Gla:
only two zebra cros:

There are a few (
for a cup of tea w

16

On Your Own

Going Shopping

1

Make a list of the things you want. If you can't read have the list in pictures or get someone to help.

2

Remember your money and your shopping bag.

5

Get a ticket for the deli queue if you need to buy cheese, bacon, sausages, ham, fish, corned beef or coleslaw.

6

Put your shopping on the moving conveyor belt at the checkout.

'Highfields' by Jill Rees

We came to Highfields on December 2nd 1974.
The staff were Peter Foulger, and Joy Swindell,
Pat, John, David and Pauline.

We started with Maxi-pak, pottery and
woodwork.

In 1976 the building was opened by Princess
Alexandra. Hazel and I have been here for 18
years.

Pottery was run by Margaret Warton. We had a
visit from some soldiers. We also went to see
the Queen opening a college in town.

Sid Hudson will be retiring in November. He has
been running Highfields for 16 years.

Mrs Winters was our first driver. Then Marie
Newth was our second. She drove the big bus.
I was an escort on the big bus then.

Dawn

Dawn is on the sm
She is a driver on
She is a helper or
Sometimes she is
Sometimes she is
Sometimes she is
Dawn is very goo

Herb Garden Word Search
by David Baldwin

M	B	P	A	R	S	L	E	Y	S	R	C
A	A	B	A	B	C	X	Y	Z	A	O	H
R	Y	A	A	E	I	O	U	R	F	S	I
J	L	S	C	A	R	I	E	F	F	E	V
O	E	I	A	V	E	R	W	R	R	M	E
R	A	L	S	M	W	I	Z	Y	O	A	S
A	F	D	A	V	I	D	W	E	N	R	R
M	W	E	Z	A	C	W	L	A	E	Y	O
E	A	S	W	D	L	E	I	D	Y	D	C
O	R	E	G	A	N	O	E	W	Z	I	K
M	I	N	T	T	H	Y	M	E	W	L	E
S	A	G	E	F	E	N	N	E	L	L	T

PARSLEY   BASIL   CHIVES
DILL   THYME   ROSEMARY
SAGE   MINT   MARJORAM
BAY LEAF   OREGANO   SAFFRON
FENNEL   ROCKET

The group have so far fund-raised to produce two books of their work. Subjects for their poems range from Elvis and drug pushers to wild dogs and tea bags. Some of their poems are reproduced below. A professional video has been made of members of the group reading their own work.

Members of the group say:

"It's nice – it's fun!"

"It's private here . . . nice and quiet."

"We gets it out of our own heads."

Elvis

Black hair combed backwards
A lip that curls up
That made the girls scream
He shook his legs
Turned his bottom hips
Blue suede shoes
Love me tender
From his sweet lips.

ALAN MARSHALL

My Face

My face
My eyes, my nose, my lips, my chin,
My neck,
Nice face, round.
Smooth flesh and hard bone.
White hair like pavements
Maud my sister, she can walk on my pavement
And angels
And the ghosts of people I've loved.
My hair covers like a stone
Covering my bone.
And my mind
Is upset because I miss those who are dead
So I let the memories of people
Walk across the pavement of my hair.

PEARL CHILCOTT

How to eat a jelly baby

Bite off their heads, their legs, chest and guts
Bite off their privates
Nothing left.
Mouth full of body pieces chewed into a thousand pieces
And they're all gone to a jelly baby heaven.

LYN MARTIN

An extract from **Brenda Mary Cook**

They said , 'You should go to a school for backward people'.
I felt disappointment and it was like an ending to me.
From then on I heard the words, 'Backward' 'Mental' 'Sick'
'Not able to do anything' 'Stupid' 'Handicapped'.
Children laughed, ganged up on me
Pulled me, pushed me
Pushed me pulled me.
Threw sticky buds at me to stick on my coat
To make me know they didn't like me
People want you to be like them
If you're not you don't fit in.

BRENDA COOK

Task sheet

► Talk to students about themes and projects they may be interested to work on and develop.

► What ideas have they come up with? Are they practical?

► How will they relate to the following:
  – Independent living skills?
  – Vocational skills?
  – Other courses the students are taking?
  – Communication skills?

► What resources would you need?

► What would the time scale be?

► What would the learning outcomes be?

Checklist

- Have you made a list of possible group work options for your group? .... ☐

  List details of:

  - the topic .... ☐
  - aims and objectives, both for the whole group and for individuals .... ☐
  - relevance/purpose .... ☐
  - materials needed

- Have you thought about how you could, where appropriate, support students to:

  - link group work to vocational skills? .... ☐
  - develop topics related to skills for independence? .... ☐
  - talk and write about their lives? .... ☐
  - remember past experiences and document them? .... ☐
  - produce a newsletter or magazine? .... ☐
  - write poetry? .... ☐

Resources

Buzz

Buzz is available by subscription to people living outside the Avon area. It is issued three times a year, and is available on tape as well as in the magazine format. Concessions are available to individuals with learning difficulties on low incomes . Details from:

Connect
Phoenix NHS Trust HQ
Stoke Lane, Stapleton
Bristol BS16 1QU

Rushlands Poets

Copies of their latest book are available. Details from:

Brenda Cook
The Portway Centre
St Bernard's Road, Shirehampton
Bristol BS11 9UR

Hortham Memories

Details from:

Val Williams
South Bristol College
The Marksbury Centre
Marksbury Road
Bedminster
Bristol BS3 5JL

Snapped Lives

Details from:

Julie Evans
Rhondda Arts
c/o Parc & Dare Theatre
Station Road
Theorchy
Rhondda CF42 6NL

Past Times

Private publication, edited by Dorothy Atkinson

Details from:

Dorothy Atkinson
School of Health, Welfare and Community Education
The Open University
Walton Hall
Milton Keynes MK7 6AA

CHAPTER 7

Evaluation, accreditation and progression

This final chapter looks at how progress in basic skills can be evaluated both by adults with learning difficulties and their tutors. It also gives an overview of accreditation options which some people may wish to pursue. Lastly, it considers the question "What next?" and looks at some routes for progression which have been taken by students with learning difficulties who have moved on from basic skills provision.

Why evaluate?

Evaluation is an essential part of the learning process for several reasons:

- It establishes whether or not learning has taken place and informs our future planning

- It gives feedback to the student about his or her progress

- It gives an opportunity to ask the student how he or she feels about what has been learnt.

Evaluation offers a time to review learning – whether that morning or that term – and a chance to analyse the results and their implications. It is a time for reflection and recording.

Reviewing learning

Review is an essential part of the learning process. It offers the opportunity for the tutor and student to reflect on the following issues:

Has learning taken place?

It will be important for you and the student to decide exactly what criteria you are going to use. For example, a student with memory difficulties may be able to name certain coins some weeks and not others. You and the student may decide that if he or she can name them for a set number of weeks in a row, this will show progress. Planning for reinforcement and repetition will be vital.

113

How do you both feel about it ?

If the student feels positive and enthusiastic about the learning that has taken place, this sense of success and achievement will be rewarding and reinforcing. If, however, the student is downcast and feels that he or she has failed, this negative feeling is bound to affect his/her attitude to future learning. Planning in small stages and offering success at each step helps to overcome the possibility of failure.

Think about how you feel too. Has the teaching gone according to plan? Do you need to revise your methods, materials or approach? Are there things you should have done differently? Are you pleased with the way things have gone, or do you have any worries or concerns that need following up?

Where to next?

Short term

Evaluation at the end of every teaching session informs short term planning and goal setting. If the student has learnt something successfully, you will need to plan the next stage of learning and to set fresh objectives. If the student has failed to learn, you will need to review your own teaching strategies. Perhaps the task was too difficult, or you didn't explain in clear enough language, or maybe the student was not sufficiently motivated . . . Stopping to review and to reflect gives you time to think through in detail what worked – and what didn't.

Longer term

Evaluation also informs longer term planning, particularly when it is carried out at the end of a piece of sustained learning such as at the mid point or end of a term or a course. Questions to ask include:

- Is the student ready to progress to a different course?

- How does the learning that has been achieved contribute towards the student's original stated long term aims?

- Is accreditation of learning a viable option?

It is important that we see evaluation as an active and dynamic process, with possibilities for change and development. All too often people with learning difficulties have been sentenced to a lifetime of basic skills tuition, without there being scope for them to move onwards and outwards from the provision.

When?

Evaluation should normally take place at the end of every session. In addition, it can be carried out at periodic intervals, such as at the end of term or the end of a course.

How?

There are a number of methods that you can use. You may want to use different techniques from time to time to stop boredom setting in for you and the students.

Record sheets

The planning learning sheet in Chapter 2 (page 31) gives room for a weekly evaluation under the heading "How I got on". Both tutor and student can put comments down. Student can dictate their thoughts if they are unable to write.

An example of the sort of form that could be used at the end of a term (or a sustained piece of learning) is shown on page 116.

Tape recording

Using a tape recorder can be a good way of getting spontaneous feedback from students who find it hard to write, but who are happy to speak into a tape recorder, either independently or interviewed by a tutor or another student.

Pictures

Some places have used pictures of sad, happy or neutral faces for students to tick to indicate their feelings about a piece of learning.

Video/photos

Especially for practical activities, a video can effectively show whether progress has been made. Photos too can record progress or achievements.

Portfolios

A portfolio can record learning achievements. It shows evidence of learning, which may include some of the following:

- Pictures, drawings or photos/video tape
- Worksheets
- Pieces of writing
- Number work
- List of books read
- Letters, stories or poems.

Portfolios offer a valuable personal record of learning for students to keep, which in itself offers a review of work done. They also have the advantage of offering a record of work towards competence based awards such as Wordpower and Numberpower.

End of term evaluation

Name .... **Date** ....

What has been most useful this term?

....

....

What do you feel better about?

....

....

What are you still worried about?

....

....

What have you enjoyed most?

....

....

What would you like to work on next term?

....

....

Options for accreditation

Accreditation offers students the chance to have their learning achievements formally recognised. Accreditation is growing in importance, largely due to the implications of the Further and Higher Education Act (1992). The Further Education Funding Council allocates funding for work listed under Schedule 2 of the Act. Courses which are eligible for funding include basic skills courses and courses in independent living and communication skills for adults with learning difficulties. The latter courses must demonstrate progression to other Schedule 2 courses, which include those leading to academic and vocational qualifications. Some students will want to and be able to have their work accredited; whereas for others it may not be a viable option, either because they choose not to, or because their level of work is not advanced enough. Here are some routes which students and tutors have pursued.

Wordpower and Numberpower

Wordpower and Numberpower are competence based and offer accreditation in literacy and numeracy respectively. There are different levels – the Foundation level has been successfully studied by a number of adults with learning difficulties.

> In one area, a booklet containing examples of work from the Wordpower course is circulated to all day centres. Staff and prospective students can then see what sort of level the work is at. The courses are offered only to those students who are judged by the tutor able to cope with the demands of the course. By targeting effectively, the best use is made of both the tutor's and the student's time. The success rate is good, largely because of the careful selection procedure. Teaching takes place in a pleasant, carpeted open learning centre, well equipped with computers. The group size is kept small (usually 4 to 6 students) so that the tutor can give individual attention and support.

Patterns for Living – Working Together

The Open University course "Working Together" is an adaptation for adults with learning difficulties of the "Patterns for Living" course. The course covers a range of topics by using video, audio tape and illustrated workbooks. An Open University certificate is available for students who choose to register for one. Communication and discussion are a central part of the course. An updated version is currently in the planning stages.

Open College Networks

The Open College Network exists in a number of parts of the country. It aims to offer access to a flexible, modular form of accreditation, which is locally designed and delivered to meet the needs of a particular group of students. Courses are vetted and validated by staff from open colleges in other areas. Aims, objectives and outcomes must be clearly set out. Level 1 includes provision for basic skills and surviving/coping skills. A notional 30 hours of study is required to obtain a credit.

> One basic skills tutor devised a programme for independent travel by public transport for adults with learning difficulties. The course was submitted for accreditation by the local Open College.

> A course called 'Answering for Yourself' has been devised in Coventry for adults with learning difficulties, which has the theme of standing up for yourself. Open College developments in this area have focused on two key areas: developing confidence and making your views known. Video is being used as one form of demonstrating progress.

National Vocational Qualifications

National Vocational Qualifications (NVQs) offer the opportunity to have work based learning validated. In some cases, adults with learning difficulties are being offered the chance to obtain elements of an NVQ if the full requirements would be hard to meet.

City and Guilds qualifications

City and Guilds courses have been successfully completed by adults with learning difficulties in a number of subjects, such as horticulture, cookery and painting/ decorating. Underpinning study of these courses with relevant basic skills support can be crucial to the success or failure of an individual with learning difficulties.

Royal Society of Arts

The RSA offers a few possibilities for accreditation which can be linked to basic skills, such as preliminary certificates in computing and keyboarding skills.

English Speaking Board

The English Speaking Board offers a range of levels of certificates for oral communication. Adults with learning difficulties have successfully passed English Speaking Board assessments, and have gained confidence in speaking up as a part of the process.

> One college offered an English Speaking Board syllabus to adults with learning difficulties. The students became noticeably more communicative and confident. They were awarded certificates, and some of the group went on to join college formal committees to represent students with learning difficulties.

Progression on from basic skills tuition

Tutors sometimes defend the idea of lifelong basic skills provision for adults with learning difficulties on the basis that if students don't come, they will regress and "go backwards". In fact, if learning is not retained or reinforced by everyday life, it is clearly not of central relevance to the student's real day to day existence. Although adults with learning difficulties have the right to develop their basic skills if they choose to do so, to expect an entitlement which is life long and entirely open ended is unrealistic. People may becoming for reasons quite unrelated to basic skills development.

George, an elderly man with learning difficulties, had been attending basic skills provision on and off for 20 years. When he returned after one of his frequent breaks, the tutor asked him why he had decided to join the group again. George replied: "Well, you see, it's lovely and warm in here!"

Opportunities for progression are important but can be difficult to access. As one tutor said: "We're under so much pressure to keep going with individuals – and there are no clear progression routes locally."

So what sort of routes have students with learning difficulties pursued after a period of basic skills tuition? Here are a few opportunities which people have followed up:

- Joining a mainstream adult education class.

Sunita had attended literacy and English for Speakers of Other Languages classes for about seven years. She decided she wanted a break from basic skills and signed up for a yoga evening class. She was delighted to meet several other Indian women at the yoga class, and has made new friends, as well as making good progress in yoga.

- Moving from a segregated group of adults with learning difficulties to an integrated basic skills class.

Christina felt ready for a change, and that she had "outgrown" her basic skills group for adults with learning difficulties. She had significantly improved her reading and writing. She had been with the members of the group for most of her life – at special school and then at the day centre. Christina was transferred at her wish to a mainstream group. She is supported by a volunteer within the group. As well as continuing to develop her literacy skills, she has developed socially. She is quite shy, but with support and encouragement, has taken a turn at making coffee for the whole group and shown others how to use a computer programme. Both achievements have given her a lot of pleasure, as well as increasing her interaction with other people in the group.

- Moving into employment.

Michael was an active member of a self advocacy and communication adult education group for adults with learning difficulties. He had to drop out when he got a job at a supermarket. He does miss the group, but relishes the new independence his job gives him. "I can buy my family presents now!"

- Moving on to education and training opportunities offered by other agencies.

> James had received 1:1 and/or group literacy tuition for about five years. The local college started to open up provision to adults with learning difficulties. James was pleased to move on to the college to take up a place on a National Vocational Qualification course in retail, complete with work experience in a shop.

- Joining a different group to study one of the accreditation or certification options such as those listed in the previous section.

> Edgar lives in a long stay hospital in the home counties. He joined a group studying the Open University "Working Together" course. He was delighted to be one of the first students nationally to complete the course, and even more pleased to be photographed receiving his Open University certificate from the OU course team.

- Joining day services offered by Health, Social Services, private or voluntary schemes.

> Catherine comes regularly to a weekly basic skills class. She spends time improving her reading and writing and has dictated several letters to relatives in Australia. Catherine was selected to join a course at the local horticultural college, which was sponsored and staffed by the local Social Services department. She is given "day release" to continue her literacy class. She is now learning words relevant to her horticulture course, such as "onions" and "seedlings".

- Progressing to do voluntary work.

> Winston gained a lot of skills in working with computers in a group for adults with learning difficulties. He left the group and moved on to become a volunteer tutor working with a computer-based basic skills group.

Sometimes people may just want to take a break from learning – as one student wrote – "I have learnt enough for now, thank you." For others, dependence on the basic skills group can be so great that it is hard to encourage people to think about moving on. In some cases, the tutors are also dependent on "their" students, and resist changes to the group. Sometimes long established groups can become little more than social clubs, with no clear focus on basic skills or progression onwards. In these cases it is unfair to expect scant basic skills resources to offer continued resourcing. Perhaps there are other ways of funding the group to meet socially, through services such as youth or leisure, or with backing from voluntary groups such as MENCAP.

In one county, a basic skills group had been meeting for 19 years. People came regularly, out of habit, but showed little motivation or progress. The decision was taken to close the group down. Counselling and guidance were offered to students about other educational options available locally. The resources which had been tied up for nearly 20 years were re-directed and new basic skills provision was offered to a fresh group of learners on a time limited basis.

Task Sheet

▶ Find out what, if any, basic skills work with adults with learning difficulties has been accredited locally. Talk to colleagues about the advantages and difficulties of various accreditation options and routes.

▶ Make a list of locally available progression routes for students with learning difficulties.

▶ How could you make this information accessible to adults with learning difficulties?

▶ What use could you make of resources such as pictures, photographs, tapes and visits to explain possible opportunities to students with learning difficulties?

▶ Research possible advice and support locally available through counselling offered by:

- Education guidance services
- Careers services
- Job centres, to include disability advisory services.

Checklist

- Have you explored possibilities for accreditation in basic skills for adults with learning difficulties? .... ☐

- Have you found out about local opportunities for progression routes for adults with learning difficulties? .... ☐

- Have you explored what support for accessing progression routes can be offered by services such as education guidance and careers? .... ☐

Accreditation: addresses for further information

Wordpower & Numberpower

City & Guilds of London Institute
76 Portland Place
London W1N 4AA
Tel: 071 278 2468

Working Together – Course P555(M)

Full details of the course and certificate are available from:
Health, Welfare & Community Education
The Open University
Walton Hall
Milton Keynes MK7 6AA
Tel: 0908 274066

Open College Networks

A key contact for Open College Networks nationally is:
Caroline Mager
Further Education Unit
Spring Gardens
Citadel Place
Tinworth Street
London SE11 5EH
Tel: 071-962 1280

National Vocational Qualifications

For general information contact:
National Council of Vocational Qualifications
222 Euston Road
London NW1 2BZ
Tel: 071 387 9898

Royal Society of Arts

Westwood Way
Coventry CV4 8HS
Tel: 0203 470033

English Speaking Board (International) Ltd

26A Princes Street
Southport PR8 1EQ
Tel: 0704 501730

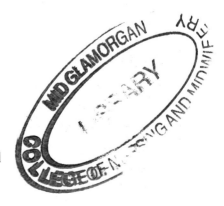

Appendix

Useful addresses

Adult Literacy & Basic Skills Unit
Commonwealth House
1-19 New Oxford Street
London WC1A 1NU
Tel: 071 405 4017

Newsletter and publications on basic skills.

British Epilepsy Association
40 Hanover Square
Leeds LS3 1BE

Practical help, counselling, public education, action groups.

British Institute of Learning Disabilities
(formerly British Institute of Mental Handicap)
Wolverhampton Road
Kidderminster
Worcestershire DY10 3PP
Tel: 0562 850251

"British Journal of Learning Disabilities" (quarterly), "Advantage" (compendium of training events produced three times a year), "Mental Handicap Research" (biannual), "Current Awareness Service" (monthly bibliography), information on courses, regional groups.

Down's Syndrome Association
153-155 Mitcham Road
Tooting
London SW17 9PG
Tel: 081 682 4001 (24 hour)

Offers information, advice, support and counselling for people with Down's Syndrome, their carers, interested professionals and others.

Further Education Unit

Spring Gardens
Citadel Place
Tinworth Street
London SE11 5EH
Tel: 071 962 1280

Publications and information relating to the development of further education.

King's Fund Centre

126 Albert Street
London NW1 7NF
Tel: 071 267 611

Publications based on health service developments for people with learning difficulties.

MENCAP National Centre

123 Golden Lane
London EC1Y 0RT
Tel: 071 454 0454

Support and help for parents, residential services; training and employment services, leisure facilities; courses for staff; legal and information services; conferences and campaigns. Publishes "MENCAP News" (monthly) and a book catalogue "MENCAP Books".

National Association of Teachers in Further and Higher Education (NATFHE)

15-27 Britannia Street
London WC1X 9JP
Tel: 081 451 1114

Trade union and professional association "NATFHE Journal", "Journal of Further & Higher Education". Specialist subject sections include special educational needs and adult basic education.

National Autistic Society

276 Willesden Lane
London NW2 5RB
Tel: 081 451 1114

Advice and guidance to professionals and families; journal "Communication"; training courses and seminars.

National Institute of Adult Continuing Education

21 De Montfort Street
Leicester LE1 7GE
Tel: 0533 551451

Advice and information on adult education, journal "Adults Learning" (monthly), publications list on request.

Norah Fry Research Centre

University of Bristol
3 Priory Road
Bristol BS8 1TX
Tel: 0272 238137

Research into services for people with learning difficulties. Details of publications and current research projects are available.

Skill: National Bureau for Student with Disabilities

336 Brixton Road
London SW9 7AA
Tel: 071 274 0565

Voluntary organisation developing opportunities for students with disabilities or learning difficulties in continuing education. Journal "Educare", publications, advice, regional groups.

Spastics Society

12 Park Crescent
London W1
Tel: 071 387 9571

Publishes "Disability Now" newspaper. Central information unit.

Values Into Action (VIA)

(formerly Campaign for People with Mental Handicaps, CMH)
Oxford House
Derbyshire Street
London E2 6HG
Tel: 071 729 5436

Newsletter, annual conference, normalisation workshops, publications.

Useful journals

Adults Learning
National Institute of Adult Continuing Education
19B De Montfort Street
Leicester LE1 7GE
Tel: 0533 551451

ALBSU Newsletter
Adult Literacy & Basic Skills Unit
7th Floor
Commonwealth House
1-19 New Oxford Street
London WC1A 1NU
Tel: 071 405 4017

Community Care
Quadrant House
The Quadrant
Sutton
Surrey SM2 5AS

Community Living
Hexagon Publishing Ltd
5 Dickerage Lane
New Malden
Surrey KT3 3RZ
Tel: 081 336 0220